THE YOUNG
WINSTON CHURCHILL

Winston Churchill was to become one of the greatest statesmen in English history, and his qualities of leadership and initiative were apparent from an early age. At school, full of mischief and energy, he was the naughtiest boy in the class. At Sandhurst, he led his fellow students in 'The Battle of the Barricades'. In South Africa during the Boer War he accomplished a headline-making escape from prison camp. And in 1901, at the age of twenty-six, Winston Churchill entered the Houses of Parliament.

THE YOUNG WINSTON CHURCHILL

John Marsh

A Lythway Book

CHIVERS PRESS
BATH

First published 1955
by
Evans Brothers
This Large Print edition published by
Chivers Press
by arrangement with
the author
1985

ISBN 0 7451 0173 9

British Library Cataloguing in Publication Data

Marsh, John, *1907*–
  The young Winston Churchill.—Large print ed.
  —(A Lythway book)
  1. Churchill, Winston S. (Winston Spencer),
  1874–1965 2. Prime ministers—Great Britain
  —Biography
  I. Title
  941.082′092′4   DA566.9

  ISBN 0–7451–0173–9

Photoset, printed and bound in Great Britain by
REDWOOD BURN LIMITED, Trowbridge, Wiltshire

CONTENTS

FOREWORD

By the Rt. Hon. L. S. Amery, C.H.

For the young generation of today Sir Winston Churchill was a majestic figure who, after forty years of active political life, was called upon to lead and inspire his country and the Empire in what he rightly called 'their finest hour'; who for another ten years after the end of the war had, as an elder statesman, continued to serve England and the cause of freedom in the world; who, at the age of 80, retired from the Prime Ministership. A life of great adventure and achievement in the political sense. But it is as well that those who are still young enough to be stirred by the call to adventure in the sense of dangers gaily sought out and overcome, of daring deeds of physical courage, of hairbreadth escapes, should be reminded that Sir Winston in his time had and enjoyed his full share of these. It is of this side of Sir Winston's life that Mr. Marsh has written. And he has asked me, as one who had known his hero from boyhood and in his days of youthful adventure, as well as over half a century of political conflict and comradeship, to add a few lines by way of foreword.

Adventures are for the adventurous. They may sometimes come to the most determinedly stay-at-home. It is always possible, in the most quiet back street, to run into a lion just escaped from a travelling circus. But, in the main, if you want adventure you must go and look for it where it is most likely to be found. As a soldier the young Churchill never missed a chance of going where fighting was going on. If there was no British war to take part in he could at any rate get his first taste of active war by joining the Spaniards in Cuba. If his regiment in India was not immediately engaged, he somehow wangled his way to the fighting frontier and, whether nominally a combatant or a war correspondent, or both simultaneously, had his fill of excitement and danger. In spite of every official attempt by Lord Kitchener to stop him he slipped out to the front in the Sudan war, again combining telegrams to the *Morning Post* with thrilling cavalry charges and the writing of a two-volume history. The same spirit took him out to the South African war both as writer and fighter.

How determined he was to never miss a chance of something happening, I can tell from my own experience. Mr. Marsh tells the full story of Churchill's gallantry in the affair of the wrecked armored train, of his capture and of his escape. But I can add something to it, which rubs in my point. I, too, was a war correspondent in that campaign and was at that moment sharing a tent with Churchill. We had both gone out once before in the armored train and had vowed not to go again, as it could see nothing, trundling along the valley bottoms, advertised its presence for miles by its puffing, and was at a hopeless disadvantage against any enemy who cared to tear up the rails behind it. However, both our ponies being lame, and forgetful of our recent vows, we decided to go with it for something to do.

The armored train, I should explain, was timed regularly to start at six, but had never previously got away before eight. So when Winston's Indian servant called us both at five-thirty and I saw that it was pouring, I protested from inside my sleeping bag that it was no possible use spending two hours getting wet at the siding only three hundred yards away. However, Winston was feeling active and offered to run across and find out. Apparently he only just caught the train, for the next thing that woke me from my peaceful slumber was the sound of gunfire a couple of hours later. I leapt up and with J. B. Atkins, the *Manchester Guardian* correspondent, ran and walked four or five miles to the scene of action. On our way we met the engine and tender, covered with wounded and unwounded refugees. They were full of praise of Winston's gallantry in helping to clear the wrecked front truck off the rails and enabling the engine to get away, and thought the rest of the troops on the train might still be holding out. This was not so, for very soon we came in sight of the wreckage, and had a distant glimpse of the main body of Boers and their prisoners disappearing over the skyline while a rearguard kept off a handful of Natal mounted men who were trying to effect a relief.

Now for the moral to add to Mr. Marsh's story. Once, many years after, when Winston and I were discussing the merits and demerits of early rising, I reminded him of our experience on that day as proving that the early worm was apt to get caught by the birds. His rejoinder was prompt: 'If I had not been early, I should not have been caught. But if I had not been caught, I could not have escaped, and my imprisonment and escape provided me with materials for lectures and a book which brought me in enough money to get into Parliament in 1900— ten years before you!'

If young Winston was undefeated he was also, as his retort to me shows, indefatigable. Every adventure was not only enjoyed for its own sake, but afforded material for articles, lectures, or a book. These in their turn were not written for the mere pleasure of speaking or writing, though I know how much he enjoyed both even in Harrow days. They were meant, both by earning money and by earning fame, to help him on with the main adventure of his life, the adventure of politics. Never to miss a chance of turning adventure, but also never to miss the chance of turning adventure to good account by sheer hard work—not a bad recipe for both enjoyment and success in life.

CHAPTER ONE

'THE NAUGHTIEST BOY IN THE WORLD!'

Down the length of the long playroom ran a trestle table, and on this were set out hundreds of lead soldiers, mounted and foot, with cannon and baggage wagons. There was a fort with carefully sited breastworks, drawbridges, and stout battlements behind which the defenders waited for the assaulting battalions. Flags flew, ambulances stood by for casualties, dispatch riders dashed about on swift horses. All was ready. The battle was joined.

Behind the table surveying the opposing forces was a small red-haired boy. His freckled cheeks were flushed, his blue eyes bright with excitement, as he reviewed the military problem before him. Then his hand stole out to the formidable gun which was trained on the attacking soldiers from the battlements of the fort.

'Fire!' he cried suddenly and watched with glee as the shot from the little gun mowed its way through the foremost soldiers coming up the slope to the fort.

'That'll teach 'em to advance in open order!' he declared, then ran to the end of the table

1

where a field piece was trained on the fort.

'Fire!' he cried again, and this time the gun's aim was not good. The tiny shot hit the side of the fort and dropped into the moat.

Other guns fired. The casualties on both sides mounted. But soon it was obvious that the attack on the fortress had failed.

'Blow the retreat!' the seven-year-old general cried, and so ended the battle.

From his earliest years Winston Leonard Spencer Churchill loved soldiering. In his eyes his great ancestor, John Churchill, first Duke of Marlborough, was the greatest soldier who ever lived. The battle which the lead soldiers in that playroom were most often called upon to fight was—Blenheim. The small boy had a soft spot in his heart for Blenheim for another reason, for it was in Blenheim Palace, the home of his grandfather, the Duke of Marlborough, that he was born.

On November 30, 1874, his parents were visiting the palace. Winston was born in a small room on the ground floor while a ball was in progress only a short distance away. Visitors to Blenheim Palace often comment adversely when the guide shows them the poky, not too well-lighted room in which on St. Andrew's Day the great man was born.

Winston Churchill, as this story opens, had recently returned to London from Ireland with his parents and baby brother Jack. There his father, Lord Randolph Churchill, had been acting as private secretary to the Viceroy, the Duke of Marlborough.

Now two important events lay almost immediately ahead. Lord Randolph was to enter Parliament; his elder son was to set off for his first school even though the term was half-finished.

The thought of going away from his home and especially from his beloved mother terrified the little boy.

Lady Randolph was the brightest star in young Winston's life. Daughter of an American newspaper owner, she had all the quality and drive which is usually associated with her race, in addition to which she was beautiful and witty. To the little boy she seemed a fairy princess, who, with the wave of her white hand, could work miracles and fill the life of all those about her with enchantment and wonder.

It is not surprising then that Winston hated the idea of leaving his comfortable home, presided over by this adored creature, for the gloom and unknown terrors of school.

The chosen establishment—it specialized in preparing boys for Eton—was situated near Ascot. Winston and his mother traveled to the station in a hansom cab.

Winston spent most of the short journey groping tearfully in the darkness for three half-crowns which, after his mother had handed them to him, he had let fall on the straw-covered floor.

St. James' School charged high fees and attracted within its walls the sons of some of the richest and noblest families in the land. Its highly colored prospectus spoke of individual tutoring, electric light (at that time few establishments boasted this), a splendid swimming pool, and every facility for the sporting boy who liked cricket and football.

But though he knew all about these wonderful things, Winston's heart was heavy as an old four-wheeler carried him and his mother through the dark November afternoon from Ascot station to the school.

The headmaster received Lady Randolph and her small son in his private quarters and made himself very pleasant during tea.

Winston tried to be brave when his mother took her leave. But when he found himself alone with the man who for the next two years was to have him completely in his power, his courage almost deserted him. Tears pricked into his eyes, tears which he brushed angrily away.

'Follow me, my boy!' the bearded giant said, drawing his gown about his ample figure and striding out of the well-furnished hallway of his own quarters into a cold passage which led into the part of the building reserved for the boys.

The rest of the school were on the football field, so the Head put Winston in charge of the man who was introduced to him as his form master.

'Have you done any Latin before?' the man asked.

'No, sir!'

'Well, study the first declension in this Latin grammar. In half an hour I will ask you to repeat it to me.'

The little boy, still sad because of his mother's departure, stared at the book almost in despair. What did these strange words mean? *Mensa*, a table, *Mensa*, O table, *Mensam*, a table. It was utter rot to him.

But one thing he was good at. He could memorize. When the master returned, his mind had photographed every word on the page.

'Well, have you done what I asked?'

'You asked me if I would study the first declension, sir.'

'Let's hear it then, boy. Don't waste time!'

Without more ado Winston gabbled off the meaningless words, and the master smiled.

'Excellent!' he cried.

If no more had been said he would probably have told his young charge to go and get warm in the Common Room. But getting to the bottom of things had got Winston into trouble before.

'What does "O table" mean, sir?' he asked with a puzzled frown.

"*Mensa*, "O table," is the vocative case,' the

5

other replied, peering rather suspiciously at the little boy to see if he was pulling his leg. 'You use it when addressing or talking to a table.'

Winston looked at him, open-mouthed.

'But I never do talk to tables,' he cried in honest amazement.

The master's brow darkened.

'You'd better be careful what you say, my lad, or you'll get a beating from the Head,' he said angrily.

If Winston's start at St. James' was unfortunate, it was nothing to the misery of the weeks that followed.

One of the headmaster's favorite pastimes was to assemble the school in the library, then singling out those to be punished, take them in turn into the next room for a thrashing. The screams of the victims did little to cheer those quaking in the other room.

Winston's health began to suffer. During the holidays he said little to his parents, who, in any case, were busy about their own affairs—Lord Randolph in Parliament, Lady Randolph in society. If he had opened his heart to them, they would no doubt have thought he was romancing.

But two years after he started his school life, his mother realized he was ill and he was taken away.

Before his purgatory ended, however, he earned himself yet another flogging and at the same time made himself the most popular boy in the school. Wrongly accused by the Head of some trifling sin, the furious Winston seized the man's straw hat, put his foot through it, and threw the pieces at the outraged bully.

Years later, still longing to give the brute who had caused so much misery a piece of his mind, Winston returned to Ascot to seek him out and denounce him before his pupils, very much as Nicholas Nickleby denounced Mr. Squeers before the boys of Dotheboys Hall. But he found that the school had closed long before and the detested headmaster had disappeared.

'And where shall we send the boy now?' Lady Randolph asked the family doctor.

'Brighton!' she was advised. 'The sea air will soon set him up again, especially if he does his lessons in pleasant surroundings and under kindly guidance.'

Winston was accordingly sent to an establishment on the south coast run by two kindly old ladies, who encouraged him to study those subjects which interested him most: English, poetry, history, and the French language. He also rode and swam to his heart's content, started a school paper which he called *The Critic*, and tried his hand at producing a pantomime, which, however, was so ambitious a production it never reached any stage.

One might have supposed, in such pleasant surroundings and under such kindly supervision, that Winston might have become less wilful and lost his rebellious high spirits which had always got him into trouble at St. James'. Not a bit of it!

His dancing mistress described him as 'a small red-headed pupil, the naughtiest boy in the class. I used to think he was the naughtiest small boy in the world.'

Once when a mistress was asking the children in the class to confess to the number of good conduct marks they had lost, Winston cried, 'Nine!'

'Nine!' gasped the mistress. 'But it would be impossible to lose so many.'

A grin appeared on the boy's freckled face.

'Nein,' he chuckled. 'I haven't lost any. I'm speaking German!'

During his stay at the school in Brighton—that is, until he went to Harrow at the age of thirteen—Winston followed his father's career with breathless interest. From the newspaper he cut all Lord Randolph's speeches, as well as any stories or cartoons which dealt with his idol, sticking them into a treasured scrapbook.

Lord Randolph was not the conventional politician. He was a man of very determined views. At the time Mr. Gladstone's Liberal administration was in power, and Lord Randolph, a Conservative, lost no time in sniping at the other side from the back benches.

'The duty of the opposition is to oppose,' he

said, and there was rarely a debate in which his voice was not heard pouring ridicule on some project put forward by the other side.

At times when he considered that his own leaders were hanging back in the attack, he turned on them, and it was often said that he had as many enemies inside his own party as outside it.

He was not popular with his opponents or his own party. Though his whole intention was to turn out the Liberals and win power for the Tories, he had inflicted many wounds on those who should have been his friends, and while they were ready to take advantage of the campaign he was waging, they smarted and longed to get their revenge on him for what they regarded as the many insults they had suffered at his hands.

Writing about his father many years later, his son said: 'To them my father seemed an intruder, an upstart, a mutineer who flouted venerable leaders and mocked at constituted authority with a mixture of aristocratic insolence and dramatic brutality.'

But he was a hero to the young Winston and to the great mass of people in the country. His meetings were always packed whenever he spoke. Cries of 'Yahoo, Randy!' and 'Give it 'em hot!' greeted him whenever he rose to his feet.

His upstanding figure, with the bulging eyes and big moustache, made him a gift to cartoonists, who usually depicted him as 'Jack the Giant Killer,' a wasp, a pug dog, a monkey, or a clown.

Lord Randolph, deep in his own affairs, had no knowledge of his eldest son's hero worship. But Winston never let slip an opportunity to reveal how big politics already bulked in his own life. Once, when bathing in a London swimming pool, he asked the attendant if he was a Whig or a Tory.

'Oh, I don't bother about politics,' the man said, whereupon his young questioner gasped in indignation.

'But you pay rates and taxes, man!' he cried. 'You should be standing on a box in Hyde Park telling people what you think about things, not taking tickets in a swimming pool!'

CHAPTER TWO

THE BOY WITH THE BOMB

A little crowd of visitors stood to one side of the schoolyard watching roll call. As the master called the names the boys filed past.

'Which is Spencer-Churchill?' several asked as boy after boy went on his way.

The red-haired boy at the very end of the line heard the words and grinned a trifle ruefully. As his name was called he went jauntily forward.

'Why, he's last of all!' someone muttered, as if quite unable to believe that the son of the famous Lord Randolph Churchill could be bottom of the whole school.

Winston Churchill's entry into Harrow at the age of thirteen caused little stir. In fact, had it not been for Mr. Welldon, the headmaster, he might never have entered the school at all.

For when he sat for the entrance examination he was completely floored by the Latin prose paper. Not one single question could he answer! After writing his name at the top of the blank sheet, he wrote down the number of the first question, carefully put a bracket round it, then brooded sadly for two hours. In that time a blot and several smudges had somehow found their way onto the clean foolscap sheet, and these in time met the critical gaze of Mr. Welldon.

Fortunately the headmaster saw more in the new boy than his failure to understand Latin. Winston was admitted to Harrow School in the summer term of 1888 and placed in the bottom form. [In 'My Early Life (p. 16) Sir Winston speaks of entering the School in 1887. This is not borne out by the Harrow School Register. Mr. L. S. Amery, too, went to Harrow in the autum of 1887 and was already high in the School when he first met Churchill at the time of the famous 'Ducker' incident in 1889.]

In this lowly position he stayed for nearly a

year. Because the English master—R. B. Somervell, father of Chief Justice Somervell—loved his subject and knew how to pass on his enthusiasm, the boy came to love the English language with a passion that remained with him through life.

Later Winston flatly refused to learn the dead languages. In his opinion Latin and Greek were a waste of time. Threats did not sway him. He let it be known quite plainly that he would only work at the things he cared for and with the masters he had taken a fancy to. Probably a little to his own astonishment, he got away with it.

Maybe the explanation was that while still in the lowest form he gained a prize open to the whole school for reciting to the headmaster twelve hundred lines of Macaulay's 'Lays of Ancient Rome' without making a single mistake; and that when he was still almost at the bottom of the school, he passed the preliminary examination for the Army, and so entered the Army class, where Greek and Latin were not all-important.

Unlike the boys who in school stories make up for their failings at lessons by brilliance at football or cricket, Winston was a duffer at most games, although he was a strong swimmer and a fine fencer. In fact, before he left Harrow he had won the Public Schools Championship with his foil.

As a new boy he went one afternoon for a

swim in the 'Ducker,' the big open-air swimming pool.

Standing with other fourteen-year-olds, he watched rather enviously some of the older boys swimming around and laughing and talking together.

At the edge of the pool stood a little chap about his own size. Evidently he was wondering whether or not to jump in. Winston decided to make his mind up for him.

Creeping cautiously forward, he raised his foot and put it in the small of the other's back, then gave a vigorous push. With a yell the other boy disappeared into the water.

Winston's friends crowded round him with concerned faces.

'You fool! Don't you know who that was?' they asked in horror. 'It was Amery. He's in the sixth form! He's head of his House!'

A few moments later Leo Amery, small of stature but high in the school, scrambled from the pool. Seizing the discomfited Churchill, he hurled him into the water and followed to give him the ducking of his life. Later, when Winston apologized, Amery forgave him and the two became friends. Years afterwards in sterner circumstances they became colleagues in governing the country.

L. S. Amery was the first editor to accept an article from Winston Churchill's pen. As a schoolboy he edited the school magazine, the

Harrovian, and one day was approached by Winston who had written an article highly critical of the school authorities responsible for a recent assault-at-arms in the gymnasium. Amery used the article though he had to blue-pencil several of the choicest witticisms in spite of the author's protests. Other articles followed, also generously blue-penciled by Amery.

As all articles in the *Harrovian* were anonymous, it must have been a shock to Winston when Dr. Welldon, the headmaster, sent for him. After observing that he had noticed certain articles that were not calculated to increase the respect of the boys for those in authority over them, he intended, if any further articles in a similar strain appeared, to swish Winston and no one else!

All schoolboys are nervous when visited by mothers and other female relatives. At Harrow at the end of the last century anguished letters would be received at home days before the expected visit, saying exactly what the lady concerned must wear and do.

And one of the strictest injunctions was that on no account—repeat! on no account—must she demonstrate her affection in any way whatsoever.

Boys have been known to waken in the middle of the night, sweating with horror in case their mothers on arrival drew them close and pressed a kiss on their crimson faces.

Yet when Mrs. Everest, Winston's old nurse, announced her intention of coming to Harrow to visit him, he merely dropped her a line saying he was looking forward to seeing her.

And when she arrived wearing a shabby old poke bonnet, her ample figure dressed in a fashion which had been out of date for years, he not only greeted her with a smacking kiss, but took her arm through his and paraded her up and down the High Street, ending by taking her into the Tuck Shop for tea!

Though Winston was a dunce at Harrow—he did not leave the Lower House the whole five years he was there—he made his mark in many ways, though some pranks did not become generally known till later in life.

'Jack,' he said one day to his friend Jack Milbanke, 'see what I've found!'

It was an extract he had copied from an ancient statute which he had dug up in the school library.

Together the two boys read it through. It soon became obvious to young Milbanke that Winston had found a way of escaping compulsory football, which they both hated.

'Does it mean that during Trials Week we needn't play footer?' asked Jack.

'Yes! Trials Week is for examinations, and this says that football might interfere with study. So—what about it?'

Seeing the mischievous twinkle in Winston's

merry eyes, Jack Milbanke nodded.

'We'll be for it if it doesn't come off—but I'm game!' he agreed.

So Winston, supported by his friend, went to the monitors and announced that as football during examination week might prove injurious to serious study, the two of them intended to abide by the ancient statute.

The whole school, when it heard, was flabbergasted and expected to learn at any moment that Winston and Jack had been dragged off for a birching by the headmaster.

But to everyone's astonishment no such thing happened. Winston and Jack were excused football, though there is no record that they studied any harder for the concession that they had been granted.

On another occasion Winston heard that there was a disused well in the grounds of an old house near the school. Rumor had it that the mansion, empty since the death of its owner nearly thirty years before, was haunted, and that a passage ran from the bottom of the well to the parish church some distance away.

After a preliminary reconnaissance Winston came to the conclusion that if he could manufacture a home-made bomb, he could clear the debris which choked the bottom of the well and so open up the passage to the church, which he would then explore.

One afternoon he left the school, and

haversack on back, made for the crumbling wall which surrounded the overgrown grounds. With a quick glance round to ensure that he was not observed, he scaled the wall and climbed down on the other side, taking great care that he did not bump the haversack in doing so.

Approaching the well, he peered into the darkness below. There was little time to lose. At any moment some busybody might take it into his head to look over the wall and see him, and then the game would be up with a vengeance.

Taking the bomb from the haversack—with a great deal of ingenuity he had earlier secured the ingredients to make it—he lit the fuse, and quickly lowered it at the end of a length of cord to the bottom of the well, retreating to a safe distance until the explosion came.

But there was only silence. Impatient, because if he was not soon back at school he would be missed, Winston went to the well and peered in. What had happened? Had the fuse gone out?

At that moment the bomb went off.

With a cry of dismay he recoiled. His eyebrows were singed; his face scorched.

Not knowing how badly hurt he was, he went back to the wall and scrambled over. A lady in a nearby house saw him. She had heard the explosion and had come to her door.

'But you've had an accident!' she cried, and taking his arm, she led him bewildered and unresisting, into her house, where she dressed his cuts and bruises and helped him to clean up.

'You're from the school, aren't you?' she asked.

Winston nodded. Now that he knew he was not badly hurt, his high spirits were uppermost once again. His merry eyes sparkled below his red hair.

'Yes, I'm from the school all right,' he said with a laugh, 'and if this gets out I'll get the bag.'

A few minutes later he hurried up the hill again. The lady, who had recognized him, smiled to herself.

So that was the famous man's son! Well, so far as she was concerned, no one would ever know of the bomb incident. She felt she owed that to such a great and admired politician, for by this time Lord Randolph was Leader of the House and Chancellor of the Exchequer in Lord Salisbury's Conservative government, which had won the General Election of 1886.

During the five years he spent at Harrow Winston Churchill made two attempts to pass into Sandhurst. After his second failure his father, not too well pleased, took him away from school and made arrangements for him to attend a crammer's establishment in London. This gentleman, a Captain James, undertook to get anyone, short of a congenital idiot, into the Army. Lord Randolph decided to give him a chance with his son, though he was not too hopeful of his success.

However, before Winston could settle down to his concentrated studies, he met with a serious accident.

While visiting some counsins at Bournemouth with his young brother, he agreed to play a game in which he would be the quarry and his cousins and brother the hunters. Making for a rustic bridge which spanned a 'chine'—a deep cleft in the cliff—he found his cousin at one end and his brother at the other.

Most boys would have laughingly given in and admitted defeat. Not Winston.

Seeing the waving tops of the young firs below, he decided to leap for it, catch the top of a fir, and slide down to the ground some thirty feet below.

Winston grasped the fir, but it did not support him, and he fell heavily to the ground. For three days, he lay unconscious and the doctors shook their heads, for he had ruptured a kidney in his heavy fall and in those days that was usually fatal.

This accident made him an invalid for nearly a year; though it was then that he met at his father's house many leading political figures of the day: Mr. Balfour, Mr. Joseph Chamberlain, Lord Rosebery, Mr. Asquith and others. Listening to these men talking together, he got his first real glimpse of the political scene. As soon as he was convalescent, he was visiting the House of Commons to listen to the debates. His father took part in these, though Lord Randolph, since his resignation some years before from high ofice, was no longer the firebrand he once had been.

CHAPTER THREE

THE BATTLE OF THE BARRICADES

At the third attempt Winston Churchill passed the Army entrance examination and entered the Royal Military College at Sandhurst.

A photograph, taken in his cadet's uniform, shows a sturdy young man with grave enquiring eyes and a mobile generous mouth which seemed likely at any moment to break into a mischievous grin.

For young Churchill had a ready sense of humor and was usually bubbling over with fun, though he was always willing to fight a losing battle for something he devoutly believed, as was the case in the famous 'Battle of the Barricades.'

In these spacious Victorian days it was the thing for the young bloods of the town to congregate together in the evenings, especially on Saturdays, at the Empire Theatre in

Leicester Square. For a long time the large space behind the dress circle, known as the Promenade, had been a meeting place, for there refreshments could be obtained.

It was decided by several members of the London County Council, led by a Mrs. Ormiston Chant, that this was wrong. A theatre was a theatre and should be used as such. Talking to one's friends and refreshing oneself at the same time was wicked and should be stopped.

Cadets from Sandhurst were allowed a brief leave in London twice a month at the weekend. When it became known that a movement was on foot to close the Empire Promenade—a favorite rendezvous—they were indignant.

Most indignant of all was Cadet Churchill.

About that time he noticed in the newspaper that had christened Mrs. Chant and her friends 'Prudes on the Prowl' that an 'Entertainments Protection League' was to be founded to hold public meetings and to enroll members to fight the good cause of freedom.

Only his military duties kept Winston from setting off to London there and then to offer his services in person. Instead he wrote a letter to the founder at the address given. Days passed before a reply came. Winston's impatience was acute. Would his offer be rejected? Would he be considered too young to give any substantial support to such a worthwhile project?

21

His fears were groundless. The letter, when it came, invited him to attend the first meeting of the newly formed organization.

The next few days were largely spent in composing a speech to be given at this first meeting.

It was a good speech. Occasionally Winston tried bits of it on his friends, who applauded in all the right places. They were almost as excited as he was about the forthcoming trip, for was he not their champion going out to fight the good fight for freedom?

At last the great day arrived. After lunch Winston changed out of his uniform and made for the railway station. On the slow journey he rehearsed again and again the main points of his speech, which by this time he had off by heart.

When the train reached Waterloo he called a hansom cab and gave the driver the name of the hotel at which the great meeting was to be held. The driver perhaps looked a little curiously at him, hearing the name, no doubt wondering what his smartly dressed young fare wanted with such a place. But Winston did not notice. His mind was full of his speech . . .

Presently the cab, which had crossed London, entered a maze of back streets behind Leicester Square and pulled up before a dingy building.

Paying off the hansom, Winston went into the

gloomy hall. A rather shifty porter asked him his business, then jerked his head toward the door of a room.

'There's a gennulman in there about that!' he said and turned back to his evening paper.

Winston opened the door indicated. A solemn individual in black rose from a chair and faced him.

'Is the first meeting of the Entertainments Protection League being held here?' the young man asked.

The other nodded and shook hands.

'I am the founder to whom you wrote,' he replied mournfully.

'I suppose you are waiting to take me up to the meeting?'

The other shook his head in a thoroughly dispirited way.

'I am afraid no one else has turned up,' he said. Then more brightly, 'Perhaps we should start. You and I can draw up a constitution and agree on procedure.'

With a sinking heart Cadet Churchill said, 'But you wrote on headed notepaper. I thought the League had already come into being.'

The other smiled shamefacedly.

'Headed notepaper only cost five shillings a box,' he said. 'I thought it would encourage . others to come forward if I had some done.'

A few minutes later Winston, boiling with indignation, his speech still in his pocket, was out in the street. So this was what you got when you tried to organize public opinion! Didn't people realize that their liberty was at stake? Suppose it had been more than an attempt to close the Empire Promenade! Suppose some foreign power was about to invade the country! Would they be as lily-livered about *that* as they were about Mrs. Ormiston Chant and her dark schemes?

As he had only half a crown in his pocket, and feeling very hungry—he had not eaten at midday—Winston forgot the affairs of the Entertainments Protection League and wondered where he could raise the price of a meal.

Seeing three golden balls hanging above a jeweler's shop in the Strand he paused. He had the gold watch his father had given him on his birthday. He should be able to raise a bit on that, then he could have the best blowout London could provide.

Opening the door, he marched in.

'How much do you want, sir?'

'A fiver!'

The money was handed over, and hanging his keys on the lightened chain, Winston went off to seek his dinner.

On his return to Sandhurst all of his friends were eager to learn how the meeting had gone. Here Winston showed his flair for diplomacy. He spoke of the difficulty of forming public opinion, of how it might be a considerable time before sufficient money could be raised to fight the stern fight that lay ahead, of the necessity to proceed step by step and be sure that the responsibility and power rested on the right shoulders—in short, he threw sufficient dust in the eyes of his colleagues to keep them quiet for the time being.

No doubt he hoped that in the days that followed the affairs of the Entertainments Protection League and his own part in it would be quietly forgotten.

But he had not done with Mrs. Ormiston Chant and the Empire Promenade!

Shortly after his disappointing visit to London, several music halls, including the Empire, decided to steer a middle course by separating the bars from the promenades by light canvas screens.

The proprietors thought this measure would meet the objections of Mrs. Chant and her followers. Though the ankles and hats of those on one side of the screens could be seen by those on the other, the two bodies of people were not technically in the same place, which was the main bone of contention.

Mrs. Chant was delighted. She had made her point. She had won her fight. In future those who wanted refreshments would be separated from those who merely wished to walk about with their friends. Life could go on.

On the first Saturday night after the screens were put up, Winston and several of his friends went to the Empire Theatre.

Other young men and women were there, too, many of them undergraduates from the universities. In fact, the famous promenade was packed to capacity.

A certain time was spent in examining the offending screens; then someone observed that perhaps a walking stick properly handled would penetrate the canvas. When the experiment was successful, Winston and his friends joined in. In a flash dozens of sticks and umbrellas had been thrust into the canvas, like pins into a pincushion.

The manager, watching from a safe distance, held his breath.

Then suddenly—it happened.

As if at a signal the crowd of young people fell on the flimsy barricades and literally tore them to pieces. The attendants were helpless and could only look on. After a very few seconds the barricades were swept away, and the two parts of the famous promenade were united as before. Men and women from each side shook hands as if they had been parted for days. Arm in arm the cheering crowd marched up and down, waving pieces of the screens to show that right had triumphed over might.

Then it was that Winston Churchill made his first public speech. Mounting on the ruined barricades, the future Prime Minister addressed the uproarious crowd, who cheered his fine phrases and sentiments to the echo.

'You have seen us tear down these barricades tonight,' he cried in ringing tones. 'See that you pull down those who are responsible for them at the coming election.'

Later he led the singing and cheering crowd into Leicester Square, waving fragments of wood and canvas so that everyone could see what a famous victory had been won.

That night he and his companions caught the last train from Waterloo, which reached Frimley, near Aldershot, at three o'clock in the morning. Here no conveyance could be found to take them on to Sandhurst, eight miles away, and as they would be in trouble if they were late on morning parade, they decided to rouse the local innkeeper.

At first there was no response to their thunderous banging and noisy shouting; then suddenly a window above the front door opened, and the landlord's head, decorated by a nightcap, appeared. In his hands was a fearsome blunderbuss, which he pointed at the group of cadets with trembling hands.

It took some time to convince him that they were not highwaymen; but at last he was prevailed on to come downstairs and harness an old horse to the ancient fly which the young men pulled from the stable.

In this Winston and half a dozen of his friends continued their journey to Camberley. By climbing a wall and taking unofficial paths through the grounds of the Military College, they arrived back in good time for parade.

The next few days were spent by Cadet Churchill in wondering if the authorities would get wind of the name of the young man who had egged on the rioters at the Empire Theatre. For his father was still famous, and the newspapers would make the most of the news if it got out. But as the days passed and nothing more was heard he began to breathe more freely.

He was disappointed to see, though, that at the county council elections, which were held a few weeks later, those in favor of erecting 'barricades' in the various musical halls were returned at the polls. Some time later walls took the place of the canvas screens, and the old Promenade at the Empire became just a treasured memory.

CHAPTER FOUR

UNDER FIRE

Winston Churchill was just twenty years of age when his father died in 1895. For many months it had been obvious that Lord Randolph was failing. Political disappointment hastened his end.

Much of his son's pleasure at passing out of Sandhurst with honors—he was eighth in his batch of one hundred and fifty—was spoiled by the death of the man who had never understood how much he loved and admired him.

Winston received the Queen's commission and was appointed to the Fourth Hussars. The first few months were spent drilling with the troopers and receiving exactly the same training as they did.

But when this period of intense activity ended, and Winston began to lead the easy life of an officer in a crack regiment—hunting, shooting, and the pleasures of the London season—he soon grew impatient.

Would there never be a war? he must often have thought. For in that year of 1895 England had not been engaged in any major conflict since the Crimean War over forty years before. There was only one small cloud on the world horizon.

That cloud gave Lieutenant Churchill an idea. He had been reading of the rebellion in Cuba against Spanish rule. One day he took his friend Reginald Barnes aside. He and Barnes had often discussed in despair their slender chances of ever winning renown in battle, and Winston now pointed out that there might be a chance of some action if only they could get to the other side of the world: to Cuba, in fact.

'But how on earth can we do that?' Barnes naturally asked.

'Well, we have five months' leave this coming winter,' Winston replied, 'so there's nothing to stop us suggesting to the Colonel that we spend it studying military tactics, and where better than in Cuba?'

Barnes, though he saw many difficulties in the way, agreed to leave things to his friend. But obstacles to Winston were things to be surmounted. Soon he had won round his commanding officer and had persuaded a friend of his father's, the British ambassador in Madrid, to get the necessary permits from the Spanish authorities.

One cold autumn day two excited young subalterns left England for New York. A month later they stood at the rail of their ship looking eagerly across the harbor toward the city of Havana.

There before their eyes was Cuba, the 'Pearl of the Antilles,' scene of the only war then being waged throughout the whole world.

The strange sights and sounds of a foreign port brought a sparkle of excitement to the eyes of the young men. Here they were, actually setting foot in the capital city of a country which was in the grip of a murderous rebellion. They were a little sorry that there were no warlike sights in Havana itself, but they knew that they must be patient. In due course they would be in the thick of the fighting.

They were received with great enthusiasm. The important letters which Winston Churchill carried put the two young men in the position of unofficial ambassadors who had come at a time of trouble to give encouragement to an old friend and ally.

They put up at a hotel, and there heard that Marshal Campos, in command of the Spanish forces charged with putting down the revolt, was upcountry inspecting garrisons which were scattered in different parts of the country.

'You will be able to join him in Santa Clara,' an official told Winston. 'You will go by armored train. If firing breaks out, all you need do is lie down. You will be quite safe.'

The journey to Santa Clara, near the center of the island, started the following morning and passed off without incident, much to the secret disappointment of the two young Englishmen.

However, when they arrived at their destination, they were welcomed by the captain-general, who put them in the charge of one of his staff officers.

'If you wish to see the fighting,' they were told, 'you should join a mobile column. One such column under General Valdez left early this morning for Sancti Spiritus, forty miles away, which is beset by the rebel forces.'

'But couldn't we go after it?' Winston asked enthusiastically. 'We should be able to

31

catch it up.'

The officer shook his head with a grim smile.

'You would be shot long before you overtook it. The rebels usually leave large bodies of men strictly alone. But two! it would be suicide.'

The two Englishmen persisted, however, and eventually they were told they could intercept General Valdez's column if they went to Sancti Spiritus on a roundabout route by train and sea.

It would take three days and involve a journey of a hundred and fifty miles; but it would be even quicker than the marching column, which, pushing through the forest, would take four days.

The two young men left at once. The journey was uneventful, for the railway line along which they traveled was strongly guarded by blockhouses. Though there were several alarms, no shots were fired, and at the scheduled time Lieutenants Churchill and Barnes reached Sancti Spiritus.

'What a filthy place,' Barnes muttered as they entered the noisy crowded tavern where they were to put up for the night.

Both young men were tired out, and in spite of hearing that there were quite a number of cases of smallpox and yellow fever among the population of the town, they slept soundly.

The following evening General Valdez and his men arrived. The column consisted of some three thousand Spanish infantrymen—fit and sturdy-looking in their cotton uniforms—with, in support, two squadrons of cavalry and a mule battery.

How eagerly must the two young officers from Britain have examined the features of those fighting men as they marched into the town, whose inhabitants had turned out in force to welcome them. The heavy packs, the double bandoliers, the dirt and dust of their journey through the jungle, made them romantic figures indeed.

General Valdez greeted Churchill and his friend cordially. He told them through an interpreter that he much appreciated their presence, which was proof positive that Great Britain approved of the Spanish attempt to bring peace and prosperity to Cuba.

'You are very kind, and we are sure that our stay with you will prove most instructive,' Winston said, and after the interpreter had passed this on, General Valdez told them to be ready at daybreak.

Next morning long before dawn the two young officers mounted their horses and joined the column, which moved off into the dark jungle. They were in uniform with loaded revolvers at their sides.

It was a great moment. They had come thousands of miles, spending money they could ill afford, to take part in a quarrel which was none of their business. Yet they did not see it that way. This was adventure. This was a climax to all the lectures, all the training, all the drills, all the field days they had endured both at Sandhurst and Aldershot in the last two years.

Naturally, as observers they would not be able to take part in any fighting except in self-defense. But at last they were part of a war. They were no longer peace-time soldiers.

When day broke, the column was deep in the forest. The rising sun, shining through the branches, lit up the dewdrops which decorated each leaf like diamonds, and outlined in all their glory the tropical fruits and flowers.

About nine o'clock open country was reached, and here breakfast was prepared over quickly lighted fires. After this it was siesta time, and the two Englishmen were invited to enter hammocks slung between the trees. This surprised the young men.

'Go to sleep for four hours in the middle of the day!' Barnes cried. 'But—what about the enemy?'

'Sounds a jolly good idea to me!' His companion chuckled. 'No doubt the rebels are fast asleep as well!'

At two o'clock all was bustle again. An hour later the column was once more on its way, much refreshed by the halt.

This was the program for several days to come. It was a most peaceful procession through a wonderful countryside, sometimes deep in the luscious forest, at other times across an open rolling landscape. And at night the campfire and the comfortable hammock, with never, after the first uncertainty, the fear of a bullet in the back or a stab in the dark.

Winston and Richard had many talks together about the difficult campaign their friends were waging in the humid forest.

'How can they expect to win?' Winston asked. 'There is no enemy for them to attack. And you just can't go on marching four thousand men round a jungle for ever.'

'And don't forget the other two hundred thousand soldiers in posts and garrisons all up and down the place as well,' his friend put in. 'Spain's a poor country. Yet either they've got to put this insurrection down or clear out of Cuba for good. Which is it cheaper to do?'

On November 29 Winston and Richard slept in the fortified village of Arroyo Blanco. Two battalions and a squadron had gone off to provision a series of garrisons in the interior. Those left—some 1,700 fighting men—were to seek the enemy and bring him to battle, if possible.

It was Winston Churchill's twenty-first birthday on November 30, and as he moved off with the rest of the column in the early morning he must have compared his present circumstances with the sort of celebrations that would have taken place if he had been at home in England.

Hardly had the column left the shelter of the fortified village than a volley rang out. There was a low mist, and Winston could see little of his immediate surroundings.

Behind came more firing as the Spaniards at the rear of the column returned the fire of the ambushers.

Presently the firing died away. Almost at the same time the mist lifted to reveal that the track had been seriously invaded by undergrowth. This needed clearing with machetes, and progress was slow until the welcome order to stop for breakfast was passed down the column.

There was no siesta in a hammock for the two British officers today. Rations were distributed and each man stood to, rifle within reach. For there was no doubt now that the enemy were all about them and likely to react violently, perhaps within minutes.

Suddenly a ragged volley rang out. Lieutenant Churchill ducked instinctively as a shot whistled past his head.

Looking round, he saw that the horse immediately behind him had been struck. Blood came from the wound in its chest. Though it did not fall, it was obviously doomed. The trooper who had ridden it so far knew this, for with a sad expression he began to take off the saddle and bridle.

'A close shave!' Barnes said as he and

Winston went on a few minutes later.

Winston nodded thoughtfully. A foot nearer, and his own corpse, not the horse's, would have stayed behind in the depths of the Cuban jungle!

All day the column wound its way through the jungle. Presently toward evening more open country was reached through which ran a pleasant river.

The weather was very hot. When camp had been made, the young Englishmen persuaded several of General Valdez's staff officers to bathe with them in a pleasant pool.

After the long ride the water was delightful, and the young men laughed and chaffed each other as they swam about.

But at last, probably enticed by the scent of cooking which came from the campfires, they left the water and started to dress.

A shot rang out, then another, then a volley. Bullets buzzed over the heads of the startled bathers like angry bees.

'Run for it!' somebody shouted, and after making sure that nobody was hit, the half-clad officers made their way back to camp.

Here a full-scale action was in progress. The rebels hidden in the forest had opened fire on the camp. The Spaniards were replying vigorously, and there were soon casualties on both sides.

This exchange lasted half an hour or so, then the rebels went off into the forest, carrying their wounded and dead with them.

That night Lieutenant Churchill found that his hammock had been slung in a little barn. He would much rather have lain on the ground, where he could have secured some cover, for the thatch walls of the barn offered little protection.

But no one else showed any desire to sleep out under the moon, so he said nothing.

Soon after retiring rifle fire broke out again, not isolated shots but sharp volleys. Bullets ripped through the thatch, and a sentry moaned as he fell.

Winston, about to abandon the hut, noticed that a stout Spanish officer was sleeping peacefully in a nearby hammock. Shrugging, he decided to stay where he was. If the Spaniard did not worry, why should he?

The column was early astir in the morning. As soon as it was on the move, rebel fire broke out again. The enemy was clearly falling back, but in doing so, was determined to make the advance of the Spaniards as costly as possible.

In full daylight the column at last reached open country from the broken ground by the river.

It was now possible to see the enemy's main position. This was on a long low hill backed by dense forest. A broad grass ride with a wire fence on one side and some stunted trees on the other ran up to it. Fields of rank grass, waist high, lay to each side of the ride, which was about a mile long and had a grove of palm trees on its right-hand side. The long low hill where the enemy was prepared to make his stand was at the end of the ride and at right angles to it.

Two companies of Spanish infantry were thrown forward on each flank and extended. The cavalry went to the right of the ride, and the artillery to the center.

General Valdez, his staff, and the two British officers rode up the ride about fifty yards behind the guns.

At first nothing happened. Except for the jingle of equipment there was no sound. Then suddenly from the distant crest came puffs of white smoke followed by the thud of the rebel's rifles.

Other volleys followed, then fire became continuous all along the enemy's line. The Spanish riflemen were also blazing away as they advanced. Soon the battle was in full swing.

General Valdez, accompanied by his staff and the British visitors, rode forward through the hail of bullets. The Spanish general, halting only some five hundred yards from the rebel position, sat his horse and watched his men go into the assault as if he was quite unconscious of the bullets which were whining about his head.

Winston Churchill cast a glance at his friend. If a Spaniard was so cool under fire, it would not do for an Englishman to show fear. So he and Lieutenant Barnes sat stiffly as if on parade, secretly hoping that the marksmanship of the Cuban insurgents would not prove any better than on the previous day and night.

But the rebels had had enough. As the Spaniards reached their positions they broke and ran into the shelter of the woods. The two Englishmen, riding up behind General Valdez, were told that as pursuit of the defeated rebels would be impossible through the dense forest, the Spanish force would be returning to the coast. Honor had been vindicated and the rebels taught a lesson at very small cost: a few horses and men wounded.

Winston and his friend were disappointed. This was a very tame ending to the adventure. However, there was nothing for them to do but accompany General Valdez back to his base.

A few days later they were on board ship once more, returning to England and their regiment. But they did not go without reward.

For on their chests were ribbons showing that they had received from the hands of General Campos himself the Spanish Order of Military Merit of the First Class. This was a matter of great envy to their fellows when they rejoined their mess at Aldershot. For in those days of profound Victorian peace, medals—especially active service medals—were as scarce as snow in August.

CHAPTER FIVE

THE NORTHWEST FRONTIER

Nine months after his Cuban adventure Winston Churchill was bound for India with his regiment. After a voyage lasting twenty-three days the troopship dropped anchor in Bombay harbor.

So eager was Winston to get ashore that as the skiff which he and two friends had hired came alongside the quay, he put out his hand to grasp an iron ring set in the stone wall.

At that moment the little boat fell away in the swell, and Winston's arm was almost dragged from its socket. This painful accident—which he made light of at the time—had a far-reaching effect on his activities in the future. It let him down on many occasions on the polo field and while swimming, and it completely brought to an end his activities on the tennis court. He could never be sure at any moment of stress that his shoulder would not give way. It was a handicap he carried through life.

Winston found India very much to his liking, and he enjoyed to the full the many sports and pursuits it offered. It was in India that during the hot period in the middle of the day, when most of his companions were asleep, he began to satisfy a desire for learning that had lately come upon him. He read history, philosophy, economics, religion, and for four or five hours each day his thirsty mind soaked in knowledge like a sponge. The glorious prose of his own writings can certainly be traced back to this self-imposed task undertaken during what he himself has described as 'the long glistening middle hours of the Indian day.'

But Winston did more than read. Up at dawn, he soldiered until noon. In the evening he played polo before dinner, then spent long pleasant hours of talk in the moonlight with his many friends.

On leave in England in 1897 he visited Goodwood. It was July and the sun beat down on the fashionable crowd gathered on the famous racecourse. The favorite had just won the principal race of the day, and the beautifully dressed women and the handsome soldierly men in the Paddock were all smiles.

A newspaper boy threaded his way through the crowd. He was selling the evening newspapers, and there was a note of urgency in his voice as he called his wares.

'War on the Northwest Frontier! Revolt of tribesmen! Paper!'

Just for a moment there was a pause in the vivacious chatter, then it went on again as the boy's voice died away across the racecourse. For a clash with ruffianly Pathans was nothing to get excited about. In any case, it was taking place thousands of miles away. It was no concern of a fashionable race crowd!

But Winston Churchill, top hat thrust to the back of his red head, stared eagerly at the paper he had bought a few seconds before, the racing banished from his mind.

So it had begun! General Sir Bindon Blood, who had successfully stormed the Malakand Pass in 1895, was taking a field force of three brigades along the Northwest Frontier of India to subdue the Pathans, who for so long had been preying on travelers on the road from Chitral to the plains of India by way of the Malakand Pass.

A companion said something, but Winston, with a muttered excuse, turned away. The racecourse, the lovely day, his companions, were forgotten.

He must get back to London. What bad luck this should happen when he was on leave! Now, instead of being on the spot, he would have to cross the world if he wanted to take part in this new war that had broken out. And the odds were that by the time he reached Peshawar, the incident would be over, and another long period of peace have descended on India.

Reaching his London home, he packed as quickly as he could. He thought again of the meeting he had had with General Sir Bindon Blood eighteen months before, when that great commander had promised him that if he ever commanded another expedition on the Indian frontier, he would take his young friend with him.

Yet he was too impatient to sit waiting for a reply to the telegram he had already sent to General Blood. He must be on his way. The sooner he reached India the sooner he would be able to pull strings at the other end and so ensure that he reached the fighting before the Pathan warriors were subdued.

Taking the train from Victoria, Winston possessed himself in patience. He had a long journey ahead of him. First the crossing to the Continent, then the train journey to Brindisi, where he would pick up the Indian mail steamer and perhaps find a reply to the telegram he had sent to General Blood.

But when he reached Brindisi, there was no reply. On to Aden. But there, in the steaming heat of the Gulf, there was still no answer.

The rest of the voyage to Bombay was torture. It was the hottest season of the year, and the hand-operated punkahs did little more than disturb the stale air in the ship's saloon.

The other passengers found the young officer very distant, almost irritable, when they approached him. They could not know that he was racked with anxiety. Would there be a telegram from General Blood at Bombay, or would he have sacrificed a fortnight's leave in vain?

Bombay had good news for Winston, however, when he jumped ashore. The general's message, whilst pointing out that things were very difficult and that there were no vacancies on his staff, advised him to come to the Frontier as a correspondent, when every endeavor would be made to fit him in.

This was enough for Winston. A correspondent! Well, why not? Already he had contributed articles to the *Daily Graphic* on his adventures in Cuba. Surely some newspaper would be able to use him as its 'war correspondent' in this new war, which, he was relieved to find, had only just started to get under way in the north.

One of the most enterprising newspapers in India at that time was the *Allahabad Pioneer*. The editor, when the young lieutenant of Hussars approached him, pronounced himself as perfectly willing to use any articles about the Malakand Field Force that were sent to him. And he would pay for them, too, though not a princely sum.

Determined to cover his expenses to the Frontier—for these would not be borne by the government—Winston cabled his mother back in England, telling her that he meant to write a series of articles and leaving it to her to fix up with a London newspaper for their publication.

He had implicit trust in his mother's ability and business sense. Always, as long as she lived,

45

he asked her advice before committing himself to any important undertaking.

It was not long before he heard from Lady Randolph that she had arranged with the editor of the *Daily Telegraph* to use his work and to pay for it at the rate of five pounds a column.

Now there was only one thing left to do. Before leaving for the Northwest Frontier, Winston still had to get his own colonel's permission for extended leave from his regiment.

His colonel was an indulgent, good-natured man. He saw how much store the young subaltern set by this invitation from General Blood and he readily gave his permission.

'The best of luck to you,' the C.O. said, and the very jubilant Winston hurried with his kit and servant to Bangalore railway station, there to get a train to Nowshera, the railhead of the Malakand Field Force, over two thousand miles away. This meant a five days' journey in the worst heat of the year.

But the heat did not worry the young officer half as much as the delay as the train steamed for five days through the baking Indian countryside. Already news was filtering back from the Frontier that Bindon Blood had come to grips with the Bunerwals, a formidable tribe, which on other occasions had resisted the British might, often with serious losses to the force sent to subdue them.

Arriving at Nowshera, Lieutenant Churchill went by tonga—pony cart—across the vast open plain some forty miles in extent to the steep road over the Malakand Pass.

Sir Bindon Blood's headquarters were at the summit of the pass. When Winston presented himself, it was to find, to his great disappointment, that the general was still away dealing with the Bunerwals.

However, in the five days that elapsed before Sir Bindon's return, Winston fitted himself out with the many necessities he needed. He bought two horses, engaged a syce (groom), and bid for several articles of clothing which had belonged to officers killed in the previous week's fighting and which were being sold by auction, as was the custom in the Anglo-Indian Army at that time.

It is necessary at this point to sketch in some details about this campaign of long ago, now overtaken and almost wiped out by the greatest events that have taken place in the present century.

For three years, since Sir Bindon Blood had first stormed the Malakand Pass in 1895, the British had held the vital road to Chitral. The tribesmen of the Chitral Valley, which lay between, resented the people who used the road, especially the foreign soldiers who came and went unmolested. Accordingly attacks were launched on the Malakand Pass garrison as well as on the little fort of Chakdara, which defended a long swinging bridge across the River Swat. The defenders of both posts had beaten the tribesmen off; guides and Bengal Lancers had chased them back along the Swat Valley, killing numbers in the process.

It was now the intention of the government to send an expedition of some 12,000 men through the mountains by way of the valleys of Dir and Bajaur, past the Mamund country, finally coming back to India and, in theory, leaving a peaceful and subdued countryside behind.

Sir Bindon Blood, returning on the fifth day after Winston Churchill's arrival at the Malakand Pass, welcomed his young friend in a kindly fashion.

'You have arrived in good time,' he said. 'You should find plenty to write about in the next few weeks.'

Winston looked at his hero with pleasure. Bindon Blood, though greatly his senior, was very much a man after his own heart. One of Sid Bindon's proudest boasts was that he was a direct descendant of the notorious Colonel Blood who in Charles II's day had tried to steal the Crown Jewels. Arrested as he left the Tower of London with an important part of the regalia under his arm, he was brought to trial. To everyone's astonishment he was acquitted and given the high office of commander of the king's bodyguard.

It was whispered that King Charles himself had put Colonel Blood up to stealing the Crown Jewels, which were to have been sold to ease his own financial difficulties.

With such a background, then, General Sir Bindon Blood was a romantic figure indeed to the young lieutenant of Hussars.

Early one morning the first brigade of British and native troops set forth from the Malakand Pass to penetrate into the valleys where for so long the law of the warlike tribesmen had held sway.

Lieutenant Churchill looked with awe at the walls of the valleys, often rising sheer six thousand feet into the crisp cold air. At the side of the narrow road ice-cold torrents roared past. There was little or no cover, and Winston had an uncomfortable feeling that hidden eyes were watching the column as it moved, like a wriggling snake, along the floor of the valley.

How easy it would be to fire on it from a thousand concealed points! For now thanks to rifle thieves and smugglers, the tribesmen were well armed with the latest weapons produced in Britain for use of the Queen's soldiers. But surprisingly enough no shots were fired, and the mouth of the Mamund Valley was reached without incident.

Here camp was made, and the English officers settled down to a pleasant leisurely dinner under the stars.

But their hopes of a quiet night were rudely shattered. As the lamps and candles flickered behind the tent canvas a number of shots rang out.

It was obvious that the Mamunds, seeing the cluster of tents and the mass of baggage animals, had not been able to resist the temptation of taking a few pot shots at them.

'What shall you do, sir?' one of the staff officers asked his chief.

Sir Bindon, continuing his dinner as if he was hardly conscious of the bullets whistling outside the tent, shrugged.

'I shall ignore their ill manners,' he said. 'The Mamunds are best left alone, at any rate at the present moment.'

So in the morning the disappointed junior officers—among them young Winston Churchill—cast a regretful eye up the Mamund Valley, where there seemed to lie the possibility of a good fight, and pressed on at the head of their men to Nawagai in the Bajaur country.

But two days later news came after General Blood to the effect that the second brigade, following behind, had been ambushed by hundreds of heavily armed tribesmen, who had caused the death or wounding of some forty officers and men and the destruction of many horses and pack animals also.

Lieutenant Churchill received orders to present himself to his commanding officer. He found Sir Bindon Blood, a dispatch in his hand, awaiting him. His eyes were stern.

'I think you're keen to get into a fight, Churchill?' he snapped.

'Yes, sir, at the earliest moment.'

Sir Bindon tersely related details of the ambushing of the second brigade.

'I have given orders to General Jeffreys that he is to enter the Mamund Valley tomorrow and seek out and punish the Mamunds. All their crops will be destroyed, their reservoirs blown up, their villages burnt. And if anyone offers resistance, he is to be shot at sight!'

'Yes, sir!'

The young officer waited tensely. Did this mean . . . ? General Blood nodded.

'An escort of Bengal Lancers is returning to the second brigade,' he said. 'You had better go with it and report to Jeffreys as soon as possible. Good luck!'

CHAPTER SIX

IN THE MAMUND VALLEY

That evening with his escort of Bengal Lancers, Lieutenant Churchill again clattered into the camp which he had never expected to see again.

Unseen marksmen on the surrounding hills

were sending a hail of bullets into the defended lines; but now the camp was surrounded by shallow trenches from which the soldiers returned the tribesmen's fire.

Churchill's party arrived unscathed. When the horses had been attended to, Winston went to get his orders for the following day.

General Jeffreys welcomed him warmly and said that the punitive expedition up the Mamund Valley would leave at first light. When it was accomplished, they would join General Sir Bindon Blood.

Though bullets flew overhead all night, the young subaltern war correspondent slept well. Before dawn his servant called him. As the eastern sky paled he was in the saddle.

The Mamund Valley was a long cultivated plain with at each side and at its end a mountain barrier. The villages—clusters of sun-baked clay huts for the most part—were strongly fortified. Some of the larger houses had battlements and drawbridges and were designed to withstand long sieges.

But as the British force—some 1,200 strong—wound its way in three sections along the floor of the valley, there was no sign of life. The three detachments of soldiers split up into still smaller parties, each setting off to hunt the unseen enemy.

Winston Churchill stayed with the cavalry, which had been given the task of sweeping to the head of the valley.

Not a shot was fired as the Lancers cantered up the broad valley between the hills with the formidable range ahead.

'Seems peaceful enough,' a young subaltern murmured to Winston.

'Too peaceful to be true!' The keen eyes looked from side to side. 'There must be hundreds of tribesmen lying hidden behind rocks and shrubs just waiting their chance.'

Suddenly there was a shout from ahead. One of the scouts was riding back. He approached the group of officers.

As he gave his report field glasses were focused on a conical hill at the end of the valley. There could plainly be seen groups of tribesmen watching the approach of the British soldiers. Seeing that a halt had been called, they commenced to wave their swords and rifles as if in defiant challenge.

A small grove of trees ahead seemed to offer suitable cover. Cantering toward it, the Lancers were ordered to dismount and engage the enemy.

A hurricane of shot from the hill answered the cavalry's carbines.

'What's the next move? We can't keep this up forever,' an officer muttered when the firing had lasted for an hour.

'The infantry will be here soon,' someone else said. 'It will be their job to carry the hill by assault.'

Watching through his field glasses, Winston presently saw the advance guard of the Thirty-fifth Sikhs toiling up the valley.

'Here they come!' he said. 'I'll leave you fellows and go on with them up the hill.'

'It'll be jolly hot on foot. Much better stick with us, old chap,' one of the officers advised.

But the young war correspondent had made his mind up. What was the use of writing about war on hearsay? He wanted to see some action, and here was as good a chance as any other.

Presently the infantry—turbaned Sikhs with English officers—came to a halt by the coppice. In a very short time the cavalry departed to guard the plain and act as liaison with the East Kent Regiment, which was being held in reserve.

Handing his horse over to a native, Winston, under a blazing sun, began to climb the hillside with the infantry. At first he crouched low, expecting a hail of bullets to greet the assault party.

But it soon became obvious that either the tribesmen, seeing the climbers, had retreated; or that they were holding their fire until presented with a better target.

The going was rough, often through high Indian corn or over boulders, sometimes along stony tracks. But with each step the summit came nearer. Winston felt that the hot blast of a volley could not now be long delayed.

But an hour after starting he stood mopping his streaming brow on the top of the mountain wall, staring back along the broad Mamund Valley lying peaceful and deserted in the hot sun.

Five white officers and eighty-five Sikhs, a little suspiciously, stood with him.

'Where have they all gone?' one officer asked.

'Sunk into the ground, as they always do,' another said bitterly. 'But they'll bob up again as soon as our backs are turned, you'll see.'

Winston examined the lush peaceful valley below. Where *was* the army? Twelve hundred men with their horses and baggage had entered this small enclosed strip at dawn. Now, except for a few dismounted Lancers far below, there was not a sight of them. The valley had swallowed them up as if they had never been.

It suddenly occurred to him that the small force, of which he was a part, was not large enough to conduct much of a fight if the tribesmen in overwhelming numbers returned.

'What happens next?' he asked the commanding officer.

'We must go on! There's a village not far away. It's our job to burn it down and all the crops growing round it.'

An order was given and the little group plodded on once more. They soon came to the village. It was merely a cluster of mud huts.

It was deserted.

Winston, an officer, and eight Sikhs lay down to cover the movements of their party, while the others advanced into the village to carry out their orders.

But before they could start the captain of the company appeared. He spoke to the subaltern in charge of the platoon of Sikhs to which Winston had attached himself.

'Stay here and cover our withdrawal,' he said.

The subaltern saluted, and as the captain vanished told his Sikhs to keep their eyes skinned if they wanted to stay alive.

Ten minutes passed.

'They must be nearly down to their fresh position,' the young lieutenant said to Winston. 'Perhaps we should go back now.'

At that moment the mountainside seemed to come to life. Smoke puffs blossomed on the hillside like white flowers, the sun glinted on wildly waving swords, flags appeared from nowhere and were vigorously waved, and a storm of bullets sang around the ears of the British soldiers.

Winston watched fascinated as the white-and-blue-clad figures of the Pathans leapt, ledge to ledge, down the mountainside, yelling and screaming as they advanced on the village.

'Open fire!' the officer ordered, and the eight Sikhs were not slow to obey.

Winston, unable to restrain his eagerness,

seized the rifle of the Sikh alongside whom he lay. The man grinned and did not try to recover the weapon. Instead he handed over the cartridges so that the young Englishman could load the rifle.

The tribesmen were now hiding behind rocks not more than a hundred yards away, but because of the accuracy of the fire from the eight rifles, they showed no eagerness to come any nearer.

'You are to retire while we give you covering fire,' he ordered. 'Get a move on! We are in a tight corner.'

The officer and seven of the Sikhs jumped up and started to go back. Only Winston and his Sikh stayed behind, for there were still seven or eight cartridges lying on the ground between the two men, and Winston knew that if they were left, they would be picked up by the tribesmen and used against British soldiers, so he insisted on the Sikh putting the bullets in his pouch.

This action probably saved his—and the man's—life; for as their comrades ran doubled up for the knoll a ragged volley rang out from the rocks. Of the eight soldiers, two were killed and three wounded, the officer included.

Just as ammunition was never left behind to fall into the hands of the tribesmen, so with the wounded. The Pathans had many unpleasant methods of despatching their victims, and every soldier in the Anglo-Indian army would hazard his own safety rather than leave his friends and comrades to their fate.

So now, seeing the officer and the Sikhs fall, the adjutant and several other soldiers came back to their assistance. With Winston and his Sikh helping, the wounded were bundled down the hill.

There was no rear guard, and inevitably the tribesmen came out of their hiding place, determined that their enemies should not slip away. Firing their rifles or waving swords, they ran toward the stumbling pathetic procession making its way to safety.

Suddenly the adjutant fell. Four soldiers lifted him up. But he was a very heavy man and their progress was slow.

With a yell of triumph several Pathans swordsmen made toward them, intent on cutting them down.

This was too much for the Sikhs carrying their officer. In a panic they let him fall and took to their heels. The unfortunate officer could do little as the leading tribesman raised his sword and slashed viciously at him.

Winston Churchill, witnessing this cold-blooded murder, saw red. Forgetting that everyone else was well on the way to safety, he turned back. The most important thing in the world was to kill the Pathan. If he did that, he would be happy.

Drawing his long cavalry sword, he moved

toward the tribesman. The man saw him coming, and bending, he picked up a small rock and threw it at the furious Winston. As this did not check the young officer, he brandished his sword and prepared for a duel. Winston hesitated. He knew he was walking into a trap. For once he became involved in swordplay with the Pathan, the man's friends would come out from their hiding-places, circle round, and cut him down at their leisure. Changing his sword into his left hand, he drew his revolver. Taking aim, he fired, but the tribesman continued to wait for him shouting defiantly. Again he fired. Once more he seemed to miss. But as for the third time he pressed the trigger, the Pathan seemed to lose his head. Turning, he ran and scrambled behind a rock.

The other tribesmen had also retreated, though from their protected position they directed their fire on the lone Englishman as he stood, smoking revolver in hand, glaring toward them.

Suddenly Winston knew that he was absolutely alone. The English officers and the Sikhs had gone. If he did not follow soon, he would be shot dead or lie wounded and helpless.

As he realized this he turned and fled for the cover of the nearest knoll. Below, he could see his friends. They waved vigorously, and very shortly he was lying panting beside them.

Carrying their wounded, the little party once

more went on its way. At each side the tribesmen stalked their prey, kneeling behind rocks and boulders to fire from time to time. Winston, arming himself with a rifle and ammunition taken from a dead man, fired back and managed to some extent to keep the exultant Pathans in check.

At the bottom of the hill a lieutenant colonel and some Sikhs waited grimly. Laying the wounded down, the survivors of the party from the hilltop joined the others standing, two deep, shoulder to shoulder, rifles presented to fire at the enemy who, now some two or three hundred strong, had crept round each flank.

'Help is near at hand,' the colonel said to Winston Churchill. 'Ride down the valley and bring them back here before we are wiped out.' But the young subaltern insisted that he gave the order in writing, for he did not want people to think, if the company was destroyed while he was absent, that he had abandoned it to its fate.

The colonel frowned, seemed about to refuse, then gave in. Scribbling a line on a piece of paper torn from his notebook, he handed it over.

'Now get on your way! There isn't a moment to be lost,' he urged.

But now an order rang out from the captain of the company.

'Volley firing! Ready, men! Fire!'

As the clustering tribesmen made as if to rush

the grimly waiting Sikhs, the rifles crashed out in a shattering volley. It was as if a scythe had torn through the ranks of the Pathans. Another volley echoed out and the Pathans turned to run. As a third volley tore into their ranks they began to retreat panic-stricken up the hillside.

'Sound the "Charge"!' was the next order, and as the bugle's exciting call rang out, the Sikhs, with a yell of triumph, went in with the bayonet.

The crisis was over. As Winston turned his horse to ride down the valley he caught sight of the leading East Kents approaching.

With the help of the reinforcements the mountain was cleared of its defenders, the body of the adjutant was recovered, and the force made its way back down the valley licking its wounds.

It was dark when Winston reached the camp from which with such high hearts twelve hundred men had set out that morning. Now they returned, tired out, leaving a score of their number behind and carrying with them a dozen wounded.

Dinner that night was an anxious meal. For the general had not returned.

Suddenly there came the sound of gunfire. This continued for some time, then there was silence.

It was obvious that the general and the half-company of sappers and miners with which he had set out were trapped somewhere in the valley.

A hurried consultation was held. But it was decided that it would be unwise to start out to rescue the general in the pitch darkness, which could only lead to disaster.

It was finally decided that the squadron of Bengal Lancers, supported by infantry, should set out to relieve the general at dawn.

Winston, tired out, lay down to snatch a few hours' sleep. Booted and spurred, he slept heavily, to be roused at dawn to find the relief column on the point of setting out.

The general and his men were soon found. They had been caught by the darkness and had decided to defend one of the valley villages rather than proceed through the darkness with the possibility of disaster overtaking them on the way back to camp.

The Mamunds had not left them in pace, launching an attack on the village under cover of the intense darkness. All night long the struggle had raged between men who knew every inch of the ground and soldiers who did not know whether they were shooting friend or foe.

Four of the ten British officers were wounded. A third of the men were casualties. Almost all the mules were dead.

Heavyhearted, the British force left the Mamund Valley. Back in camp General Jeffreys sent a message by heliograph from the top of a mountain to his superior officer in Nawagai. Back came Sir Bindon Blood's answer.

'Lay waste with fire and sword the Mamund Valley!'

Thereafter, systematically and with great care, the Anglo-Indian force went from village to village, destroying the houses, filling up the wells, and cutting down the trees and crops.

The tribesmen resisted fiercely, and there were many casualties among the officers and men committed to this policy of destruction.

'Whether it was worth it I cannot tell,' Winston Churchill wrote later. 'At any rate, at the end of a fortnight the valley was a desert, and honor was satisfied.'

CHAPTER SEVEN

BEFORE THE BATTLE

After the Malakand Field Force had done its work, Winston Churchill returned to Bangalore to regimental duties. But maneuvers and the fighting of mock battles seemed very tame after the grim happenings in the Mamund Valley.

At this time the government decided to dispatch an expedition against the rebellious Afridis in the Tirah, a mountainous region north of Peshawar and east of the Khyber Pass.

For some time this tribe had been joining in the Northwest Frontier revolt, and a considerable expeditionary force of some 35,000 men left for the Tirah Maidan, a cultivated plain the center of enemy country. The order was given that the houses, herds, and grain stores of the Afridis were to be destroyed. The Afridis themselves were to be driven into the mountains and left to perish in the snow and freezing winds.

High peaks guarded the approach to the Maidan, and the English soldiers, if they reached their objective, would be the first to do so. The prospect of the expedition excited Winston. He longed to join it.

But it was not to be. In spite of all his appeals for help from his influential friends he still found himself kicking his heels as the Tirah Expedition, after completing its task, withdrew through the mountains with tribesmen sniping from every ridge.

Sure that in the spring another expedition would leave to subdue the still rebellious Afridis, Winston pursued his attempts to go with it. But though he managed to get himself appointed to the staff of Sir William Lockhart, the commander-in-chief, in Peshawar, it was only to hear after a few weeks that peace had been negotiated and that the government would be sending no more expensive expeditions into the mountains for the present.

During this period of enforced inactivity he

wrote two books. The first, describing his adventures with the Malakand Field Force, was based on the anonymous letters which he had earlier sent to the *Daily Telegraph*. His mother placed the book with a publisher, and when it appeared, it was a big success, earning its young author praise from many famous people, among them the Prince of Wales (later King Edward VII). He also turned his hand to fiction, and *Savrola* came out, first as a serial story in *Macmillan's Magazine*, then as a book.

But the life of a literary man, even when there were regimental duties to attend to and a great deal of polo to play as well, was not enough for the active Winston.

For a long time now he had been eagerly reading about the campaign in the Sudan against the Dervishes, who, since the murder of General Gordon in Khartoum in 1885, had controlled that vast territory south of Egypt. Now that the enemy was at last having reverses, and the Anglo-Egyptian army was heading for Khartoum, Winston was eager to be in at the kill.

Taking advantage of a period of leave, he left for London in the spring of 1898.

He decided that he would approach Sir Herbert Kitchener, Sirdar of the Egyptian Army, and try to get an appointment on his staff. In that way he would be able to take an active part as a soldier in the campaign in the

Sudan and also send back dispatches to a London newspaper as before.

But things were not to go as smoothly with Kitchener as they had gone with such old friends as General Sir Bindon Blood. In spite of the fact that he had applied successfully for extended leave from his regiment, and had the approval of the War Office in his projected plans, Kitchener proved actively hostile. He quickly showed himself to be on the side of those who for some time now had been saying quite openly that Winston could do with a period of discipline and routine, and that it was not the thing for a young subaltern to be newspaper correspondent and soldier at one and the same time.

But Winston was not cast down by this rebuff. Though Kitchner had told him and his friends on several occasions that he had all the young officers he required, he explored all the chances of finding some means of transferring himself from London to Egypt and that before it was too late.

For it was now the end of June, and Kitchener's attack on the Dervish stronghold could not be long delayed.

Then quite by chance he learned through a mutual friend that the War Office was not at all pleased at Kitchener's rather highhanded method of choosing or rejecting officers of their recommendation. Winston was not slow to pass on the information that he had made several attempts to join the expedition, and that even his father's old friend Lord Salisbury, the Prime Minister, had been coldly rebuffed by Kitchener when he had wired the Sirdar on his behalf.

Two days later Winston got an order from the War Office to say that he had been appointed to the Twenty-first Lancers and that he was to proceed to the Abassiyel Barracks, Cairo, at once. No explanation was given as to how this change in the situation had come about. But the young man did not care. He had got what he wanted.

The next day, after fixing up with the *Morning Post* for a series of articles on the campaign, he caught a train for Marseilles. Six days later he was in Cairo.

In August 1898 the fight to recover the Sudan was entering its final stages. Since two Egyptian armies under British leadership had been destroyed at El Obeid and Tokar in 1884, the Sudan had been under the rule of their conqueror, a fanatical Mohammedan known as the Mahdi.

Two attempts to relieve General Gordon, shut up in Khartoum with an army of English and Egyptians, failed, and when finally a column got through, it was to find the Mahdi's flag flying over the city and Gordon dead after a heroic defense.

In the next ten years a strong Egyptian army of 15,000 men with English officers was raised, and in the many clashes with the Dervishes, gave a good account of themselves. In 1896 Sir Herbert Kitchener was appointed Sirdar, or commander-in-chief, and ordered to reconquer the Sudan in stages.

Two years of grim fighting followed, and it was not until the summer of 1897, after Dongola, three hundred miles from Khartoum, had been occupied and the Dervishes driven back in disorder, that the British government committed itself to an all-out attempt to push on to Khartoum and bring the Mahdi's successor, the Khalifa Abdullah, to battle.

When Winston reached Egypt, Kitchener had 26,000 men under his command. These, apart from the Twenty-first Lancers, included units of the Howitzer Battery and the Royal Artillery with battalions from the Warwickshires, the Seaforth Highlanders, the Cameron Highlanders, the Grenadier Guards, and other famous British regiments. Egyptian and Sudanese troops constituted the greater part of the force. A naval flotilla on the Nile advanced on the flank of the army and used its guns to good effect when the battle was joined.

On arrival in Cairo Winston found that two squadrons of the Twenty-first Lancers had already left for the Sudan. The other two were about to start, but many long faces greeted the young Englishman when he reported for duty. For rumors that the battle was due to start, if it had not already started, had been filtering back for several hours. Which if true meant that they would all arrive when the excitement was over.

Winston was almost mad with anxiety, especially when he learned that one of the troops which had already gone ahead had been reserved for him. When he had not turned up, it had been given to Second Lieutenant Robert Grenfell, who had been highly delighted to be chosen.

'Fancy how lucky I am,' Grenfell wrote to his family. 'Here I have got the troop that would have been Winston's, and we are to be the first to start.'

In the fighting this particular troop, under its gallant young leader, was practically cut to pieces. Grenfell was one of the only three officers killed in the main battle. Had Winston led this ill-fated troop it is likely that he, not Grenfell, would have fallen to a Dervish spear.

The day after Winston's arrival the remaining two squadrons of the Twenty-first Lancers set forth on their 1,400-mile journey into the Sudan. They traveled up the Nile by steamer, covering the last four hundred miles across the desert on the military railway that had been lately built as the Khalifa's forces fell back. A fortnight after leaving Cairo they joined the main army and found to their relief that they were still in time for the impending decisive clash.

Perhaps the journey was not as happy a one for the young British officer as it was for his lighthearted companions. For no hint of the Sirdar's reaction to the news that he was on his way to join the army had reached him. It would indeed be heartbreaking if Kitchener on some pretext ordered him back to Cairo, thus ensuring that he missed the impending battle.

But the blow did not fall, and Winston began to realize that perhaps the Sirdar, with the responsibility of a major engagement before him, had more to do with his time than worry about an insignificant subaltern of twenty-four.

Actually, Kitchener, hearing that the War Office had appointed Winston against his wishes, had merely shrugged his shoulders and forgotten all about the incident.

Omdurman, which finally ended the power of the Khalifa, was the last of the great set-piece battles. It was also the forerunner of future battles where mere numbers ceased to count, and where the better-armed soldier was the master of any number of ill-armed opponents.

This can be seen from the fact that at the Battle of Omdurman British losses were 3 officers and 25 other ranks killed and 145 wounded. Dervish losses were 10,800 killed and 16,000 wounded. In addition the Anglo-Egyptian army took nearly 4,000 prisoners.

Another startling fact is that of the British casualties, 21 men lost their lives and 40 were wounded in the charge made by the Twenty-first Lancers, in which Winston Churchill took part. So the rest of the British army suffered only 109 casualties in all, 4 of them fatal!

When Winston and his companions caught up with the main army, there were still several days' marching before them. It was not until August 28 that the Anglo-Egyptian force set off on the last stage of its long journey, which had brought it from the headwaters of the Nile to the deserts of the Sudan.

The heat was intense and the marching soldiers suffered considerably. Though they were never out of sight of water—for the Nile flowed within a mile—the canvas water bags could only be filled in the evenings and most had been drained by early afternoon.

The British soldier is ever a pessimist, and as mile succeeded mile and nothing more offensive than a distant horseman on the skyline was seen, many a grumble was heard that the expedition was a waste of time and that the Dervishes were a figment of the Sirdar's imagination.

But on September 1, when Winston rode out as usual with his troops on patrol duty, he halted his men at the top of a sand dune to see that the advanced patrols, which had been thrown out to guard against any surprise attack, had halted as if uncertain.

'What is it?' Winston asked a fellow subaltern, but his companion was as puzzled as he was.

But he soon learned what was afoot. A galloping cavalryman from the patrol in front shouted as he passed, 'Enemy in sight!' and there was a thrill of excitement in his voice.

'Where?' Winston cried.

But the other, pointing back the way he had come, went on his way. Winston, determined to know the truth, stopped a regimental sergeant-major who came trotting back from the outpost line.

'How many are there, sergeant-major?'

'A good army, sir,' the other replied. 'Quite a good army.'

'What now?' Winston wondered, then stiffened as his name was called.

'Yes, sir?' he cried and cantered up to his squadron leader's side.

'The colonel needs a subaltern whose horse is not exhausted. Don't delay, Mr. Churchill!'

A moment later Winston was putting spurs to his horse and making for the outpost line. Saluting the colonel, he awaited his orders.

'The enemy has just begun to advance,' he was told. 'They are coming on pretty fast. When you have seen the situation for yourself, go back as quickly as you can and report personally to the Sirdar. He is marching with the infantry.'

For a moment Winston felt a tremor of

apprehension. So he was to come face to face with Kitchener after all, was he? Well, at least the Sirdar could hardly send him back to Cairo at this late hour with the battle about to begin. In any case, he might not even be curious enough to inquire the name of the officer reporting back from the patrol.

After taking a good look at the advancing enemy, Winston rode back across the six miles of desert which separated the outpost line from the main army. It was very hot and he did not press his horse, for it was quite on the cards that his mount would have to carry him for the rest of the day, perhaps into the thick of the battle.

Topping the crest of a hill, he paused to look at the British and Egyptian army as it advanced in all its magnificence and power below. Something told him that perhaps this was the last time in history that it would ever be possible to see such an array deployed on such a scale.

In open columns five solid brigades of several infantry battalions marched toward him. Behind came long rows of artillery, followed by the camel train. On the Nile were sailing boats towed by paddle steamers and guarded by several white gunboats ready for action. Away on the other flank were squadrons of Egyptian cavalry and the colorful columns of the Camel Corps.

At the head of the infantry Kitchener rode alone, slightly ahead of his headquarters staff above which floated the Union Jack and the Egyptian flag. Winston, a little overcome by this magnificence, approached as respectfully as he could and saluted smartly.

'Sir,' said Winston, 'I have a report from the cavalry screen.'

Kitchener's grave face, with its heavy moustache and drooping eyelids, expressed neither surprise nor any particular interest. Nodding slightly, he waited for the young man to continue.

Winston, as clearly as he could, explained the situation as he had witnessed it from the outpost line.

'The enemy is almost directly between here and the city of Omdurman, sir,' he said. 'Until eleven o'clock they remained stationary, but about forty-five minutes ago they began to move forward again.'

Kitchener listened in silence, then at last he asked, 'So the Dervish army is advancing! How long do you think I have got?'

'At least an hour, sir—probably an hour and a half.'

Kitchener greeted this calculation with another nod, then turned away. The young subaltern, glad to escape, fell back, making anxious calculations. Yet if the Dervish host jogged forward for seven miles, the time he had worked out must be about correct.

Winston's fears of what Kitchener might say

to him when he knew who he was were set at rest when, invited to join the staff at luncheon, he was presented to the great man. Kitchener received him kindly and made no reference to past unpleasantness.

The army had now halted, and Winston was able to see the preparations that were being made for the coming battle.

Thornbushes were cut down and formed into an impassable barricade behind which the infantry was deployed. Winston watched eagerly for the first sign of the Khalifa's advancing forces. But he was disappointed. Soon news came that the Dervishes had halted and were unlikely to attack that day, September 1.

Later Winston rejoined his companions in the outpost line, where, after a long spell of patrol duty, he obeyed the order to seek shelter inside the zariba of thorns.

That night he slept lightly, for at any moment he expected to hear the thunder of horses and the shrill cries of 60,000 attacking men. But the night passed peacefully, and when dawn came, Winston was again on his horse riding out on patrol.

CHAPTER EIGHT

A CAVALRY CHARGE

Winston Churchill's eye was the first to fall on the Dervish army on the morning of September 2, 1898.

Sitting his horse on the ridge of the hill running down to the river, he waited for the mist to clear before the rising sun.

At first he thought that the Khalifa's men had faded away in the night, for, below, the plain seemed empty. As the light grew he saw what appeared to be dark smears against the desert sand. Then he knew that they were men, masses of men, the sun glinting on their weapons, and that they were moving toward him.

After sending a message back to the commander in chief, Winston ordered his patrol to approach even closer to the advancing host. He could hear a roar from 60,000 throats, could see in the strong light of the rising sun the glittering weapons, the hundreds of multicolored flags waving in the breeze.

Four hundred yards from this human sea, which extended over a front of four to five miles, Winston's puny force opened fire. But the bullets made no impression on the marching horde. Winston knew then that the time had come to return to the safety of the zariba.

Even as they prepared to move off, an order came from the chief of staff for the patrol to remain as long as possible and report on the movements of the enemy. Winston with his men remained on the ridge for nearly half an hour more, constantly reporting back to headquarters. Most of the Dervishes passed out of sight beyond a high point on the hill to the right, but a force of some six thousand men made up the slope toward the British patrol.

It was a wonderful viewpoint, for not only could the young officer see the enemy; he could also see the British army behind him, with, on the Nile, the gunboats ready to go into action at a second's notice.

It occurred to him that if he was not recalled, he might stay where he was during the battle. In this way he would be able to see the conflict from both sides, which would be a great advantage when writing about it afterward.

Keeping a wary eye on the nearest Dervish force, and seeing that they were not now making directly for him and his small force, he gazed awestruck at the amazing sight which surrounded him.

Suddenly several of the British and Egyptian batteries and all the gunboats opened fire on the Khalifa's men, who had now appeared over the ridge of the hills which shielded the British position.

These guns inflicted terrible slaughter. Winston and his men were so close that they could feel the blast from the bursting shells.

The brave array of gaily colored warriors with their flags and banners began to melt under the merciless pounding. Men turned to escape. Soon heaps of corpses impeded the progress of those in the rear.

Yet the Dervish army had no thought of retreat. On it streamed, banners flying, toward the British lines where in disciplined ranks the British and Egyptian troops waited behind their impenetrable thorn barricade.

Now Winston noticed that several Dervish horsemen had slipped away from the main body and were making toward his patrol. Drawing his pistol, he fired at the leading man, who wheeled away out of range, followed by his companions.

This disturbing maneuver decided Winston that the time had come to edge back toward the Nile, which would enable him to stay outside the zariba without endangering the lives of his men.

But this hope was short-lived. For an order arrived from his superior officer insisting that he regain the zariba before the infantry opened fire. A few minutes later he and his men were safe behind the thorn fence.

While the attack on the zariba developed, the Twenty-first Lancers sheltered under the overhanging riverbank. Their turn would come later. Yet in spite of flying bullets Winston raised his head to witness the carnage that followed, as the Khalifa's army came over the ridge and swept down toward the defended position.

'Poor beggars, their troubles is all afore them,' he heard an admiring British Tommy say just before rifle fire from two and a half divisions of trained infantry struck them. At the same time massed artillery pumped shells into the human wall. In less than a minute the proud host had withered away under the merciless fire.

Here and there it was possible to witness incredible acts of heroism among the Dervishes, who for the most part were armed only with spears and out-of-date rifles.

One man, bearing forward a black flag, the emblem of the Khalifa's brother, Yahoob, seemed to possess a charmed life. Though a terrific fire of infantry and artillery was aimed in his direction, he continued to advance, apparently unperturbed.

All around his comrades were mowed down, yet he stood erect and unarmed, proudly supporting his standard, his face turned toward the enemy. For several minutes he defied the hail of bullets, but at last his time came.

As he sank slowly to the ground his master's standard continued to float proudly over his mangled body, for his last act had been to drive the staff firmly into the ground.

When the attack of the Dervish spearmen was repulsed, their riflemen lay down and began to fire on the British and Egyptian lines. But this phase of the fighting did not last long.

Kitchener, seeing how the attack had been beaten off, decided to march on Omdurman without delay. He intended to cut off the remnants of the Khalifa's forces from their base and drive them out into the desert, there to die or surrender.

In spite of the slaughter before the zariba the Dervish army was still a very active force. Much of it had not even been under fire, having maneuvered too far out in the desert. In addition, the Khalifa's reserves of some 15,000 men were still impatiently waiting to go into action.

As the British and Egyptian troops left the safety of their fortified position and advanced along the bank of the Nile, these enormous forces now entered the struggle against them.

It was a critical moment. But Kitchener was not caught napping. Skilled disciplined troops, murderous rifle and artillery fire, again met the yelling mob as it closed in.

In a very short space of time the dark-skinned army melted away under a hail of shot and shell. The dead in their long white garments were piled high like snowdrifts. Those who by a miracle were still alive streamed away into the temporary safety of the desert.

During this second attack the Twenty-first Lancers were guarding the left flank of the advance on Omdurman, while the Egyptian cavalry and the Camel Corps were away over to the right.

Winston and his brother officers were impatient. They had seen the defeat of the Dervish army, and they began to fear that they were not even to make one charge to justify their presence on the battlefield.

Soon they were moving forward in columns of troops—the sixteen troops in the regiment following one behind the other—and crossing the ridge of the hills on which Winston some time before had observed the advancing Dervish army. Six or seven miles ahead of them, its minarets and domes shining in the strong sunlight, lay Omdurman. There, most sacred of all in Dervish eyes, stood the Mahdi's tomb.

Winston's troop of some twenty Lancers was the second from the rear. As they went forward Winston peered ahead. Surely there must be some chance of action soon. The way to Omdurman could not have been left entirely unguarded.

As the trumpet sounded 'Trot,' he noticed a long line of motionless figures some three hundred yards away. As the long column of Lancers advanced rifle fire broke out. Several cavalrymen fell.

It was now obvious to the colonel in charge

that if his men were not to be picked off one by one, he would have to engage the enemy without delay. The trumpet sounded, the sixteen troops wheeled into line, and three hundred crack cavalrymen, lances couched, urged their horses into a gallop.

Winston was riding a sure-footed gray Arab polo pony. Like the other officers, he had been marching with drawn sword in hand, but as he broke into a gallop he decided to sheath his sword and use the Mauser pistol he had recently purchased in London. Memories of the time when, landing at Bombay, he had badly wrenched his shoulder, determined him in his choice. It would never do to find his arm useless if in a fight for life he had to rely on his sword.

The rifle fire from the Dervishes redoubled as the Lancers swept down on them. But so loud was the thunder of hoofs and the shouts of the excited cavalrymen that any other sound was completely drowned. Only white puffs of smoke showed that bullets were winging toward the advancing Lancers.

As the charging horses swept down on the line of riflemen, Winston saw behind them a nullah, a depression in the ground rather like the dry bed of a river. And this shallow sunken little valley was crammed with Dervishes who, leaping to their feet, waved their weapons in defiance. At the same moment colored standards were hoisted high above the heads of the Emirs on horseback who commanded their humbler foot followers.

There was no time to change course now. The Twenty-first Lancers were committed to attacking an army, not a few stragglers. And unlike the rest of Kitchener's force, they could not rely on shot and shell to blast this mass of fighting men out of their path.

There were three hundred disciplined mounted men against a fanatical force ten times their size. And their weapons were no better than their opponents'. For the first time that day all the advantage lay with the enemy.

Winston's pony, reaching the edge of the nullah, checked for a moment, then dropped sure-footed down the four or five feet to the bottom of the dry river bed. In a moment he and his companions were surrounded by dozens of yelling black men all with one idea in their minds: to pull them from their horses and slash them to death.

A desperate fight took place, the Dervishes stabbing and hacking at the troopers trying to force a passage through the serried mass. Frantic hands clutched at Winston's reins, but his game little mount struggled forward, and reaching the side of the nullah, scrambled up to the level of the desert again.

Behind him was a scene of wild confusion. Further up the watercourse, where the enemy was packed more tightly, a terrible fight was in progress. Though Winston did not know it at the time, it was here that his friend Robert Grenfell, leading the troop that should have been his, was pulled from his horse and stabbed to death. Because of the press of the enemy at this point Grenfell's men had been brought to a standstill. It was the work of but a few seconds to drag the troopers from their horses and stab or club them to death.

As Winston looked round for his own men one of the Dervishes threw himself on the ground at his pony's feet. At first Winston thought he was terrified, then, seeing the flash of the curved sword, realized he was about to hamstring his mount. Leaning over he shot the man dead. Even as he straightened in the saddle another man ran at him. Again he fired, again his would-be assailant fell.

Suddenly Winston realized that he was alone. Within a hundred yards he could see no sign of officer or man of the Twenty-first Lancers, only frenzied Dervishes running here and there, shaking their spears and firing their rifles either into the air or in his direction.

Fear crept over him. Until that moment in the heat of action he had not thought about his own safety. Now he had visions of being surrounded, dragged from his horse, and mercilessly butchered. As several of the enemy made toward him he put spurs to his game little pony in the hope that he was heading in the right direction.

A few seconds later he came across his troop. They were delighted to see him and reported that their casualties had been light: four missing, and half a dozen men and perhaps ten horses bleeding from spear thrusts.

With Winston at their head they trotted over to join other troops reforming close by.

As they waited for orders, keeping a wary eye open for any attack by the watching Dervishes, who had withdrawn a couple of hundred yards, Winston asked his second sergeant if he had enjoyed the charge.

'Well, I don't say I exactly enjoyed it, sir,' the man replied amid laughter, 'but I think I'll get used to it next time.'

Suddenly from the dry watercourse came a pathetic procession of horses and men. Many were at the point of death from the most terrible wounds. Some troopers, having lost their horses, were staggering aimlessly about on foot, blood pouring from their heads and bodies, others led their horses, whose bodies had been slashed in the most terrible fashion.

After doing what they could for these casualties, the colonel decided against another charge. Instead he ordered the men to draw their carbines and proceed toward the nullah once more. Taking up a favorable position, the order was given to fire, and so accurate was the men's aim that the Dervishes were in headlong retreat.

Twenty minutes after the charge had begun the Twenty-first Lancers were in possession of the field. Out of the 310 officers and men who took part, five officers and sixty-five men were killed or wounded. One hundred and twenty were lost.

The action was watched from the river by the commander of one of the gunboats, a young naval officer called Beatty. Later, when Winston Churchill was First Lord of the Admiralty in the First World War, and Beatty was the youngest admiral in the Royal Navy, Winston asked for the other's impression of the charge.

'What did it look like?' he asked.

'It looked,' said Admiral Beatty, 'like plum duff; brown currants scattered about in a great deal of suet.'

CHAPTER NINE

A DIFFERENT SORT OF FIGHT

Winston Churchill did not stay long in the Sudan after the defeat of the Khalifa's army. After entering Omdurman and Khartoum with the victorious Anglo-Egyptian army and taking part in mopping-up operations, which cost the

Khalifa's men another four hundred casualties, he started homeward with the Twenty-first Lancers.

Much of the journey was spent in one of the big sailing boats on the Nile, where his time was largely occupied in writing dispatches about the battle for the *Morning Post*.

In Cairo he had his first experience of skin grafting. A friend of his had been severely wounded by a sword cut above the right wrist. He was now traveling to England in charge of a nurse, and Winston said he would accompany him on the journey.

However, a doctor, examining the wound in Cairo, decided that a skin graft must be made without delay. He asked the nurse if she would submit to having a piece of skin taken from her arm so that this could be placed over the wound.

The nurse agreed, but Winston, who was present, could see that she did not relish the operation, which would have to be carried out there and then without an anesthetic. The doctor also had noticed her pale cheeks and frightened eyes. He turned to the young subaltern.

'What about you?' he asked.

There was no escape. Winston, with pounding heart, drew back his sleeve and bared his flesh. The doctor, an Irishman, grinned as he stepped forward, razor in hand.

'Ye've heard of a man being flayed aloive?' he

chuckled. 'Well, this is what it feels loike.'

Thereupon he started to remove a piece of skin and flesh about the size of a shilling from the inside of the young man's forearm.

It was an ordeal that Winston never wanted to repeat. But he managed to hold on without even a groan escaping him, and a few minutes later he had the satisfaction of seeing a piece of his living flesh grafted on to his friend's wound, which quickly healed. He himself bore a scar the rest of his life.

Arriving back in England, Winston began to think seriously about his future. Though he had been in the army for over three years, he was earning only fourteen shillings a day. True enough, this was augmented by the allowance of five hundred pounds a year which his mother, in spite of her own straitened circumstances, was still giving him. Even so, it was not enough to meet the ordinary expenses of a cavalary officer who was also keen on polo and must therefore stable and feed at least two mounts.

Reviewing his literary labors he found that in the previous three years, thanks to the sales of books and articles, he had made about five times as much money as he had received as a soldier.

He decided, therefore, after returning to India to play in the Inter-Regimental Polo Tournament, to send in his papers and return to England as a civilian. He would then see if he could make ends meet as journalist and author.

By living at home he could keep down his expenses and perhaps make a go of it. He could even dispense with the allowance he had been receiving from his mother.

But before he returned to India, he found himself in great demand at the dinner table, in clubs, in any gathering where were people eager to hear of his experiences on the Northwest Frontier and in the Sudan. He also met politicians, who questioned him closely on his experiences. In fact, so much interest was shown in him that he began to wonder if, perhaps, there might not be a career for him in politics also.

He even went so far as to visit Conservative party headquarters to see if any constituency would care to adopt him as its candidate. When it was learned that he had no private means, and would not be able to pay out big sums in subscriptions and to charities if he was adopted, he was not encouraged, though he was told that his father's name and his own experiences in two wars would count in his favor when the names of possible candidates came up for review for one of the 'forlorn hope' seats.

On the way out from this interview Winston spotted a large book on a table. Its title was *Speakers Wanted.* On inquiry he learned that all up and down the country were bazaars, rallies, meetings of one sort and another, all urgently needing practiced speakers.

Before he left the building, he was booked to address a gathering of the Primrose League in Bath ten days ahead.

He spent many hours preparing a speech which would glorify the Tory party and throw scorn on the Liberals. When he traveled down to Bath, he was accompanied by a reporter from the *Morning Post.*

The speech was delivered in a big park outside Bath. Surrounded by coconut shies, booths, and roundabouts, Winston was introduced to the audience, several hundred strong, as the son of one of the greatest leaders the Conservative party had ever had, and as a hero returned from the wars.

A little ill at ease—for if this got back to his regiment, Winston knew he would never hear the end of it—the young officer rose to speak. He was delighted at the ease with which he delivered his oration. Many of his nicely rounded phrases were greeted with cheering and applause. Best of all he noticed that the *Morning Post* reporter was industriously taking down word for word everything he said.

The following day the newspaper printed the speech almost in full. In a leading article it announced that a new figure had arrived on the political scene.

Delighted to have done so well, Winston said good-bye to his mother and left once more for India.

As he had hoped, he was a member of the winning team which won the Inter-Regimental Tournament of 1899, in spite of the fact that four days before the final he slipped on a stone staircase and put his shoulder out. He played with his elbow strapped to his side, but still managed to give a good account of himself.

Soon after this, having resigned his commission, Winston was homeward bound once again. He had now begun to write his account of the campaign in the Sudan, which he called *The River War*. Always interested in other writers, he struck up a friendship on the ship with G. W. Steevens, special correspondent of the *Daily Mail*, later to become famous for his reports on the opening battles of the Boer War. He died of typhoid at Ladysmith in February 1900.

Steevens was interested to hear about the half-finished book. One day, when Winston was at work in the ship's saloon, he came in and stood behind the young man's shoulder, reading as he wrote.

Winston was proud of what he had written. He had come to a point where the Nile column had just by a forced march reached Aby Hamed and was about to storm it.

'Within this stern amphitheatre one of the minor dramas of the war was now to be enacted,' he wrote rather pompously.

'Ha! Ha!' said Steevens at his shoulder.

Throwing down his pen, Winston jumped up. He was furious.

'Finish it yourself, then!' he cried and stormed on deck.

When he came down he looked at the sheet of paper, half hoping in spite of his anger to see a valuable contribution from the pen of this famous writer.

But all Steevens had written in his small hand were the words: 'Pop-pop! pop-pop! Pop! Pop!' finishing up at the bottom of the page with a large printed 'BANG!'

But in spite of this Steevens thought enough of Winston Churchill at that time to discuss seriously with him the book he was writing and listen with interest to his ambitious plans for the future.

Back in England Winston spent his time writing *The River War* and enjoying the London season now in full swing.

One day he received a summons to the House of Commons. The Conservative member for Oldham, Mr. Robert Ascroft, explained to the expectant young man that his constituency had two members of Parliament, both Conservatives. Unfortunately, Mr. Ascroft's colleague was ill, and it seemed to Mr. Ascroft that it would be as well if he looked round for a suitable candidate immediately, in case a by-election had to be fought without too much warning. It seemed to him, from what he had heard, that Winston—because of his famous father and his exploits as a soldier-correspondent—was the very man.

Highly delighted, Winston agreed to visit Oldham in the near future and address a meeting of local Conservatives who would then 'look him over'; but a few weeks later it was Ascroft himself who died suddenly, not his fellow M.P. about whom he had been so concerned!

The government—in view of the surviving member's illness—then decided to fight both seats at once, and as the Oldham Conservatives had already expressed their willingness to support Winston's candidature, he was formally invited to stand.

The young man was almost wild with excitement as shortly afterward he journeyed to Lancashire to prepare for his campaign. The Oldham voters *must* vote for him! Why, the men that would be put up against him were only stodgy businessmen. Surely, surely, the enlightened cotton operatives of Lancashire would prefer a dashing, colorful figure who could prove to them that Tory democracy was the finest thing in the wide world!

He found Oldham in a ferment. All the cranks in the country seemed to have descended on the little Lancashire cotton town. There were anti-vivisectionists, anti-dog muzzlers, anti-this, and anti-that, all pointing out how important *their* votes were going to be when the counting started.

Winston soon met the man who was to stand with him against the two Liberals who opposed them. He was Mr. James Mawdsley, the much respected secretary of the Operative Spinners' Association. Mr. Mawdsley was a Socialist who had announced his admiration of Tory democracy. The local Conservative Association, believing that his candidature would secure many working-class votes, had adopted him along with the young aristocrat from London.

Things did not quite work out in the way that the local Conservatives wished. The working class turned on Mr. Mawdsley and accused him of letting his own side down. Many bitter and some slanderous things were said, and at an early meeting Winston, who had been greatly taken by the simple, good-hearted Mr. Mawdsley, said, 'I hear today that an anonymous pamphlet has been issued attacking Mr. Mawdsley in the foulest terms.' With blazing eyes he went on, 'If the author can be discovered, he will be liable to imprisonment without the option of a fine!'

Thus early in the election did he declare to the world that he was not going to hear his humble colleague abused without showing that he was whole-heartedly on his side.

'The Conservatives have never had a finer fighting candidate than Mr. Winston Spencer

Churchill,' wrote the editorial writer of the *Morning Post* a few days before the election. 'The Radicals have been hard put to it to find weapons with which to attack him. His brief past has been brilliant and honorable, and in their dire extremity they have actually fallen back on his youth and urged from their platforms his few years as a serious reason why the people of Oldham should not send him to Parliament.'

The young candidate was never under any illusions about the fight he was waging. Oldham was what is termed a 'swing of the pendulum' seat. In 1885 it had returned a Liberal and a Tory member, in 1886 two Tories, in 1892 two Liberals, and in 1895 two Tories again. By the law of averages it was the turn of the Liberals again.

Winston well knew that when a powerful government, such as Lord Salisbury's administration, had been in office many years the people were inclined to want a change.

But even if he suspected that he was waging a hopeless fight, he did not spare himself. His enthusiasm infected his own supporters and won for him many friends even among his opponents.

It is possible that he might just have scraped home; but early in the campaign a Mr. George Whiteley, Conservative M.P. for Stockport, a neighboring constituency, did the government's cause great harm by resigning from the party over an attempt by the Unionists to give poor clergy a dole from the land, a measure known as the Clerical Tithes Bill. Mr. Whiteley, in leaving the party, said he did so because he was 'sick and sore of the government.'

This news burst like a bomb in Oldham. That such a well-known man—almost a local man—should discredit the government in such a way! Winston's supporters were aghast; his opponents fell on the tidbit like wolves, and soon all Oldham was plastered with posters announcing that even Tory M.P.s were 'sick and sore of the government,' so surely the Oldham electorate was!

But Winston found his campaign uphill work for other reasons. In spite of the fact that there were some 40,000 unvaccinated babies in Oldham, he declared himself to be 'a stern believer in the benefits of vaccination.' In this he was supporting the government, but it undoubtedly lost him a large number of votes among the population, which looked upon vaccination as a newfangled thing the doctors had thought up for their own profit.

Great enthusiasm was shown at the eve of the Poll Rally organized by the Conservatives. The Empire Theatre, which held four thousand people, was not big enough to take all who sought admission, so the Theatre Royal near by, which could take another three thousand, was used for an overflow meeting.

Lady Randolph Churchill was on the platform. She had thrown herself wholeheartedly into her son's campaign and had made several speeches on his behalf.

Winston told his audience that he and his colleague had tried their best to fight a fair fight. After pointing out how trade had improved under the Unionist government, and how Oldham in particular had felt the benefit of this revival, he added with a boyish grin and twinkle, 'Even the death rate in Oldham has fallen since the government took office!' Referring to his opponents, he said, 'The other horses were perhaps trained a little better than ours—at any rate they made the running. But when we came into the straight and the judge's box was in view, the noble animal of Tory democracy responded to the call that was made on him, and coming up with a rush at the finish, he has made it definitely certain that we shall win.'

On the day of the poll all Oldham was bedecked with red or blue favors. Though the Liberals proudly announced that they had more conveyances to get their voters to the poll—they claimed 130 carriages against 90—the Tories, not to be outdone, called on a fire engine to help them out, bedecking it with streamers of blue ribbon!

But even the fire engine could not sway the

result, which that night was announced as follows:

Emmott (L) 12,976
Runciman (L) 12,770
Churchill (C) 11,477
Mawdsley (C) 11,449

Winston was the first to congratulate his conquerors. Mr. Emmott was an industrialist well known in the neighborhood. Walter Runciman, four years Winston's senior, was the son of a rich shipping family. Later he was to rise high in politics alongside the young Conservative he had beaten.

The newspapers were loud in their praise of Winston's gallant fight on the day following the election. The *Morning Post* summed up a fairly general opinion when its editorial writer wrote:

'Though Mr. Emmott and Mr. Runciman have come out at the top of the poll, the honors of the day undoubtedly go to Mr. Churchill. His gallant contest in a constituency to which he was personally a stranger has been followed with keen interest throughout the country, as much for the sake of Mr. Churchill's future as in memory of his late father, and the brilliant manner in which he has acquitted himself during the most interesting by-election to this Parliament makes the question of his entry into the House one of the few certainties of political life.'

Interviewed by a journalist about the result, Winston used a topical simile: 'In regard to organization I can only say that from the very first it was a case of Dervishes against Kitchener's army. We were full of enthusiasm and desperate courage on our side, but we had no organization.'

Back in London Winston turned to the correction of the proofs of his book on the Sudan campaign. In it, no longer being under military discipline, he had attacked Kitchener for desecrating the Mahdi's tomb and carrying off the Mahdi's head in a kerosene can as a trophy. Already these incidents had roused the Liberals to a loud outcry in Parliament, and as he was in effect taking their side in the matter, Winston expected some criticism from the men he was supposed to support politically.

He waited eagerly for the book to appear. Would it be as successful as *The Malakand Field Force?* Or would it disappoint those who had admired the former work?

But before *The River War* appeared, much was to happen. It was the autumn of 1899, and the Boers had issued an ultimatum demanding that British troops must retire from the borders of the [Boer] Republic. It was but a matter of days before war broke out.

CHAPTER TEN

BOUND FOR SOUTH AFRICA

The two young men faced each other across the big desk. Oliver Borthwick, good-looking, debonair, son of the proprietor of the *Morning Post*, did not waste words.

'I want you to leave for Cape Town at the earliest moment,' he said. 'The *Dunottar Castle* sails on the eleventh.'

Winston Churchill's eyes danced with pleasurable excitement. 'You're asking me to be special correspondent of the *Morning Post* to report the coming war for you?'

'Yes! And we're prepared to pay you two hundred and fifty pounds a month, plus all expenses, with a four months' guarantee. It's probably more than any war correspondent has ever been paid before.'

'It's certainly very handsome! I hope I'll be worth it.'

'I think you will! You'll do it, then?'

'Certainly!' Winston thrust out his hand and the two men sealed the bargain. 'And now I'll be off. I've a lot to do if I'm to sail for the Cape within a week!'

Out in the street Winston felt to be walking on air. Though he knew that his earlier reports on the Sudan campaign had pleased the editor of the *Morning Post,* he had had no idea that such a plum as this would drop into his lap.

Instantly all his plans for the immediate future were pushed to the back of his mind. Balls, dinners, political speeches—how tame these seemed now, though they had pleased him well enough a short time before.

He was off to the war. Pray heaven it lasted until the *Dunottar Castle* crossed to the other side of the world.

In the days of preparation that followed, he found time to brush up his knowledge of all that had happened in the last few years to worsen the relations between Briton and Boer and had led to the present situation in South Africa.

He recalled with a thrill Dr. Jameson's famous raid into Boer territory three years before which had roused the two Boer republics of Transvaal and the Orange Free State to fiery anger and redoubled the injustices against the Outlanders—English settlers in Boer territory— whom Jameson had intended to help. He reread the newspapers of the last few months and saw for the first time how the Boers had been preparing for war long before the British authorities, at home and in Cape Colony, had taken them seriously.

After reading the news that the Boers had invaded Natal and were making for Cape Colony itself, Winston embarked on the *Dunottar*

Castle. It was October 11, 1899.

He found that he was to have distinguished company on the voyage. General Sir Redvers Buller, V.C., and his headquarters staff were also aboard the vessel. General Buller was to command the British Army Corps being sent out to South Africa to reinforce the 27,000 British troops already there. Winston, eager to be sending back a dispatch to the *Morning Post*, approached the famous man and asked his views about the coming war.

But Buller had nothing to say. In fact, Buller did not seem particularly interested in the war to which the *Dunottar Castle* was steaming. He contented himself with solitary tramps up and down the deck, deep in thought. He did not even seem disturbed at the prospect of three weeks of the slow-moving liner, which, in spite of the urgency of the situation, never increased its pace above the normal cruising speed.

Winston was almost frantic with impatience. There was of course no wireless in those days, so as long as the ship was at sea no news reached it of what was going on in South Africa. Even at Madeira, which they reached on the fourth day, the only news was that though troops on both sides were maneuvering, there had as yet been no major clash.

It was almost more than the young man could bear to see his companions, as the ship sailed on under cloudless skies, disporting themselves at the usual sports and deck games. It was as if he had imagined the war, as if he had dreamed that Oliver Borthwick had engaged him as war correspondent, as if he was merely an idler who had joined a pleasure cruise through the Mediterranean. . . .

Then one day something happened to jerk everyone out of their complacency. A ship was sighted heading toward them. It was the first vessel that had been seen for several days. It was almost certain that those on board would have up-to-date news of what was happening in South Africa.

It was suggested to General Buller that he send orders to the other ship to stop and send someone aboard the *Dunottar Castle* with the latest newspapers. But Buller was a cautious man. He did not want to get into trouble for stopping a ship on the high seas. If there was a claim against the government, he might be held responsible.

However, at the prompting of his staff, he agreed that signals might be made on his behalf asking for news.

The approaching ship—she was a small tramp steamer—immediately altered course when her captain received the signal. Soon he was steaming past the *Dunottar Castle* little more than a hundred yards away.

Winston, with the rest of the ship's company, stood at the rail gazing across at the tramp as she wallowed past.

A blackboard had been fixed up so that all on the liner could see it. Crudely scrawled on it in chalk was the following message:

BOERS DEFEATED
THREE BATTLES
PENN SYMONS KILLED

This news, though full of excitement, left those aboard the *Dunottar Castle* sunk in gloom.

So the Boers were defeated after three battles, which had obviously cost the British forces casualties. For hadn't General Penn Symons been killed?

Winston paced the deck. His thoughts were in a turmoil. Did this mean that as soon as he reached Cape Town, he would be recalled? Did it mean that the Boer farmers had been driven back into their homeland and now were suing for peace? If they had been defeated in three battles, they would hardly be able to carry on against the might of the countries of the British Empire, whose trained armies were even now hurrying to enter the fight.

He sought out the gloomy group which surrounded General Buller. What must the great man be thinking now? What misery he must be suffering after seeing his chances of glory recede almost to vanishing point?

He heard a staff officer address Sir Redvers,

'It looks as if it will all be over when we get there, sir!'

The general shrugged and thought a moment before replying.

'Oh, I daresay there will be enough left to give us a fight outside Pretoria,' he said, naming the Boer capital.

Instantly everyone's morale was restored. If General Buller thought the war would still be prospering when the *Dunottar Castle* reached Cape Town, that was enough.

When Winston pointed out that he would have felt happier if the little tramp steamer had been stopped and its crew questioned, his words did little to lessen the high spirits which the general's pronouncement had released.

Twenty days after leaving England Winston landed at Cape Town. Bad news met him.

A fortnight or so before the Boers had invaded Natal, and though defeated at Talana Hill, had killed General Penn Symons and sent his force of some four thousand men in retreat to Ladysmith. At Elandslaagte General Sir George White, after a small success, had overreached himself. Nearly 1,200 British soldiers had surrendered at Nicholson's Neck, the rest hastily falling back on Ladysmith. Here the disciplined forces that should have been withdrawing southward across the Tugela, contesting every yard of the way and thus giving time for reinforcements to come up from the

Cape to attack the Boers and drive on Pretoria, were now besieged and useless inside Ladysmith.

The Boers had swept on, locking up two other forces in Mafeking and Kimberley. The despised little army of Boer farmers had suddenly become a monster that threatened to devour the whole of British South Africa.

Winston Churchill in his capacity as a war correspondent was eager to move upcountry. It was becoming obvious that the big battles lay ahead, and that they would take place not in Boer country but in Natal.

He soon realized that Buller's army corps would take about six weeks to assemble before it could march north to help the beleaguered garrisons and come to grips with the Boers. He therefore decided to go ahead, see what was happening in Natal, and return to Cape Town in time to join the main advance.

As travel through the Orange Free State was impossible, a roundabout route to Durban had to be taken. This involved a sea trip from East London in a small mailboat. The weather was very bad, and Winston suffered agonies of seasickness before landing at Durban to travel on, weak and shaky, through the night to Pietermaritzburg. . . .

Interviewing wounded in the hospital there, he found his friend Reggie Barnes with a wound in the thigh. Barnes told him all about the fighting at Elandslaagte station, in which he had taken part, and he spoke enthusiastically of the Boer as a fighting man, giving his questioner a clear picture of the skill with which the bearded farmers handled their horses and rifles.

Later Winston traveled on to Estcourt, beyond which the trains had ceased to run north toward Ladysmith.

It was his intention to try to get into Ladysmith, but he soon found he was too late. The Boers had occupied Colenso station, a few miles away, and they also held the iron railway bridge over the river.

Winston heard that General French and his staff had only just left under artillery fire on the last train out of Ladysmith and were now on their way back to Cape Colony, where the main cavalry reinforcements were assembling.

There was only one thing for the young correspondent to do. He would stay with the handful of troops guarding Estcourt station and hope that the Boers would be so occupied with the siege of Ladysmith that they would not trouble them.

At Estcourt was a single battalion of the Dublin Fusiliers, a few squadrons of Natal Carabineers, two companies of Durban Light Infantry, and two or three guns. There was also an armored train. . . .

For a week this little force remained on guard, expecting at any moment to be attacked.

The time hung heavily for Winston, though he had been much cheered to meet once again Leo Amery, who years before he had pushed into the swimming pool at Harrow. Amery was acting as war correspondent for the *Times*, and he and Winston found that they had much in common.

Then one morning the general in command of the troops in Estcourt decided he would send the armored train along the line toward the Boer position to see what information was to be gained.

The train consisted of six armored trucks. A company of Dublin Fusiliers and a company of the Durban Light Infantry would garrison it, as well as some sailors with a small six-pounder naval gun.

Winston knew the officer who was to be in charge of this expedition. He was a Captain Haldane, whom he had first met in India.

Haldane asked Winston and J. B. Atkins, correspondent of the *Manchester Guardian*, to accompany his party on the train. Atkins shook his head. He thought it was a crazy idea to venture so far into enemy territory in a cumbersome train that could be cut off from its base by the removal of a line or the blowing up a bridge.

'My instructions are to follow the British army and report what it is doing, not to get taken prisoner and spend the rest of the war in a prison camp,' he said.

Winston, though he agreed with this sentiment, nevertheless accepted Haldane's invitation to go on the armored train.

'I have a feeling, a sort of intuition, that if I go something will come of it,' he said. 'It's illogical, I know, but—well, there it is!'

How right his instinct was! That armored train led straight to fame and fortune, though the road was no easy one, as the young war correspondent found in the weeks to come.

CHAPTER ELEVEN

THE ARMORED TRAIN

The armored train looked indestructible as it stood, squat and bulky, on the line outside Estcourt station. Steam was up, and the engine driver, a little pale from excitement, glanced impatiently at the soldiers climbing into the steel-plated trucks in front of and behind him.

There were six such trucks, three behind the engine, three in front. The rear truck contained a number of footplate men in case there was any obstruction of the line. Ahead and immediately behind the tender were two trucks containing the Durban Light Infantry. In the two trucks in front of the engine were the Dublin Fusiliers. In the front truck of all were the sailors with their six-pounder.

It was a most imposing cavalcade, and those who saw it leave must have thought the Boers would never dare attack it. Winston traveled with Captain Haldane and the sailors in the front armored truck, and as the train proceeded without hindrance along the track both young men swept the surrounding hills with their field glasses.

They got as far as Chieveley station, fourteen miles from their starting point, without seeing any sign of the enemy. Here Haldane left Winston in the train and went to telegraph back his report to the general in Estcourt.

Winston swept the hilly countryside with his glasses. Suddenly his heart quickened. For on a hill just over a quarter of a mile away—a hill which commanded the railway line which led back to their base—had appeared some moving figures.

'Haldane, come quickly!' he called.

His friend wasted no time. A moment later he was peering anxiously through his own glasses at the men in the distance.

'This is it!' he muttered. 'There's not a moment to lose if we're to get back safely to Estcourt.'

An order was given and the train set off on the return journey. Winston and his companion, now in the rear truck, held their breath. Had the

Boers had time to do anything to the line? Might they not even yet get past this danger point and so regain safety?

The answer came from the top of the hill. There were several flashes, then a succession of explosions.

Winston, who had been standing on a box so that he could see above the side of the steel-plated truck, ducked as the shrapnel burst above the train. There was a dull clanging sound as the slivers of shell struck the train's armor.

At this point the railway line curved as the steep gradient took it through a cutting past the base of the hill from which the Boers were firing. The train's speed increased, and the cumbersome monster swayed madly from side to side as the driver urged it past the danger point.

It occurred to Winston, as the guns were left behind, that the Boers were hardly likely to let them get away so easily. Surely they would have laid some trap further on. He was about to voice his misgivings to Haldane, and suggest that an order be sent to the engine driver to reduce speed, when there was a tremendous impact which threw everybody in the train into a heap.

Something had been placed on the line, and the train had charged into it at forty miles an hour!

Getting to his feet Winston looked around. Nobody in his truck was more than badly shaken. He peeped over the top of the plating.

Almost at once a spatter of rifle fire came from the hill. The Boers, running over the crest, had flung themselves down in the long grass and were now directing a murderous fire on those in the derailed train below.

Haldane and Winston hastily debated what had better be done.

'If I go to the front of the train and see what's happened,' Winston suggested, 'the Fusiliers and the naval gun could give me covering fire.'

Haldane made no objection, and as Winston climbed hurriedly over the side of the truck the soldiers opened rapid fire on the Boers commanding the cutting. The six-pounder soon found the range and lobbed shells into the long grass at the top of the hill.

Just for a moment Winston hung over the side of the truck. Bullets bounced like hailstone all around him, but by a miracle he dropped to the track unscathed.

He was now in the shelter of the train. Crouching almost double, he ran toward the engine, which, to his relief, he found still firmly on the rails. The driver waved to him to show he was all right, and he ran on.

The two armored trucks which the engine and tender had been pushing before them were both off the line, one still upright, the other on its side. Jammed against each other, they blocked the way to safety for the rest of the train. The soldiers they had carried, some badly injured, were now sheltering behind them.

The men in the very first truck of all had suffered most. This had overturned after striking a shell placed on the line, and the platelayers it had carried had been killed or terribly injured.

As Winston retraced his steps another burst of shrapnel raked the train. The young war correspondent saw the engine driver, blood streaming down his face, leap from his engine and make for the shelter of the overturned trucks.

'I'm a civilian!' he cried as Winston came up and told him to return to his post. 'I drive engines. I'm not paid to be killed by a shell.'

Winston's heart sank. There was just a faint chance that they might yet escape if the engine and the other trucks could get past the obstruction on the line; but only if the driver kept his head and obeyed orders coolly.

Though every instinct urged him to grab the man by the shoulder and force him back to his engine, he reasoned with him.

'No man is ever hit twice on the same day,' he said. 'Besides, you look a gallant sort of chap. It's very likely that you'll win a medal for your part in this action, even if you are a civilian. Why, man, you might never have another chance of fame as good as this, however long you live.'

The man, who was getting over the shock of his injury, pulled himself together.

'I daresay you're right,' he murmured. Wiping the blood off his face, he went slowly back to his engine.

Winston, with a sigh of relief at the successful outcome of his diplomacy, returned to the rear truck, where Haldane's men were still keeping the Boers' heads down with accurate rifle fire. There he conferred with his friend through a loophole in the side of the truck.

'I think it might be possible to push the two trucks which are blocking the line away with the engine,' he said, after explaining the situation.

'Haven't the Boers pulled up a line or damaged the track in some other way?' Haldane asked.

'Not as far as I can see! If I have the engine driver's cooperation and good covering fire from your men, it should be possible to clear the line in half an hour or so.'

Haldane assured him that this would be done, and Winston returned to the overturned trucks to put his plan into operation.

In the next hour he bore a charmed life as he strode up and down the line, mostly in full view of the Boers, giving orders to the engine driver and directing the activities of the soldiers from the overturned trucks.

His plan was a simple one. If the truck which lay partly across the rails could be separated from the one which was clear of the rails, it might be possible—by using the engine—to push past.

Winston explained to the driver exactly what he wanted him to do. He had already uncoupled the wreck of the truck which had been thrown clear of the line, and at his signal, the engine began to drag the other partly derailed truck backward.

At first it seemed as if the engine had taken on more than it could manage. Its wheels skidded on the track, and the dead weight of the steel truck lay immovable across the sleepers.

Then suddenly the engine moved back, the truck following. The battle was half-won.

Winston now called for volunteers from the men of the Durban Light Infantry who had been sheltering from the rifle fire from above. He wanted them to help in throwing the truck clear of the line.

There was an immediate response. Twenty men stepped forward.

'Now, lads, as the engine pushes from the end, overturn the truck from your side!' Winston cried.

Giving a signal to the driver, he held his breath to see if the maneuver would be successful.

It was. With a crash the truck fell over on its side away from the track. It seemed as if the way was clear for the train to proceed back to

115

Estcourt.

But a bitter disappointment was in store. Because the footplate of the engine was about six inches wider than the tender, it caught the corner of the newly overturned truck.

At first Winston told the driver to urge his engine into the obstruction and try to butt it out of the way. But unfortunately the truck, in its new position, now had its end wedged against the other truck, which lay clear of the line. The more the engine pushed the greater was the resistance. At last a halt was called lest the engine itself be derailed.

Winston now decided, after a consultation with his helpers, to try and pull the truck away from the one against which it was jammed. But to his disappointment, when he tried to fix the coupling chains to the engine to the truck, they were found to be a few inches short.

The fire from the Boers on the hill was redoubled as they saw that the British party was making such strenuous efforts to escape. Winston knew that though he and his helpers had had most of the luck so far, it could not last much longer. Sooner or later they must be struck down.

Then someone cheered as a soldier came down the train carrying another coupling chain which he had found. This was passed from the engine to the overturned truck, and once more the driver put his locomotive in reverse.

116

Everyone held their breath. Would it move? Would the way be cleared?

Inch by inch the engine drew the truck away from the wreckage of the other. But the strain was too much for the coupling which suddenly snapped.

'It might be enough!' Winston cried, perspiration pouring down his begrimed face, his eyes strained and anxious.

But alas! when the engine went forward, its footplate once again caught the corner of the truck.

It seemed as if there was nothing for it but to tell Haldane that the train must be abandoned. That would mean either submitting tamely as prisoners of war to the Boers, or fighting a hopeless action in the cutting with the guns and rifles of the hidden enemy trained on them.

Winston gritted his teeth. No! He'd make one more attempt. If they were to abandon the train in any case, it wouldn't really matter if the engine *was* derailed. He'd launch the engine at the obstruction and see what happened.

The Boers had now opened fire from the other side of the track, and there was little protection from the storm of bullets. Ordering the men to take what shelter they could, Winston gave another order to the engine driver.

'Go back as far as you can—then let her rip,' he said.

The man looked doubtful for a moment, then he grinned.

'Yes, sir!' he said, and pulled a lever which sent the engine into reverse.

Winston waited in an agony of suspense. Had he done the right thing? Should they have made one more effort to heave the truck out of the way?

Then he saw the engine tearing toward them, smoke pouring from its funnel. He held his breath as it hit the corner of the overturned truck.

There was a loud crash, a moment when it seemed that the engine must fall over on its side, then by a miracle the truck reared upright and fell back, leaving the sturdy locomotive still on the rails, its driver looking back at Winston in triumph.

'We've done it!' the young man cried in delight.

He went back to Haldane and his men who were still engaging the Boers on the surrounding hills as fiercely as ever.

'The engine's through,' he said. 'The problem now is to get your trucks up to it and couple them on again.'

'Can't you bring the engine back?' Haldane asked, knowing how heavy the trucks were and how exposed any party called on to haul them would be.

Winston shook his red head.

'I daren't risk it!' he said. 'The truck is only just clear of the line. Though the trucks will slip past without trouble, the engine might not, then we'd be worse off than ever.'

Haldane did not hesitate. If they must push the trucks, the sooner they started the better. Giving a sharp order, he tumbled out on to the track ahead of his men.

As the soldiers began to bend their tired backs to their task the Boer fire redoubled. For now there was no return fire and bullets rattled furiously against the steel-plated sides of the truck.

It was hard going. Inch by inch the heavy, cumbersome trucks moved along the rails. But as one or two men were hit, their companions tended to make for the less exposed side of the line, which meant that the power applied by the men's shoulders was unequally distributed.

It was not long before the trucks came to a dead stop. Haldane looked at Winston in despair.

'It's no good!' he said. 'We'll never get the trucks up to the engine at this rate.'

'Then let's send the engine slowly ahead carrying the wounded,' Winston suggested. 'Those who can walk can follow in the engine's wake.'

Haldane agreed that this would be best, and the next quarter of an hour was spent in helping the wounded aboard the engine. More than forty people crowded on to the footplate and tender, and Winston, hardly able to move, stood among them directing the driver while Haldane and his men straggled along the line behind.

The Boers, seeing that their quarry seemed likely to escape after all, redoubled their fire. Shells burst overhead. Shrapnel began to take its toll.

The engine driver, in spite of Winston's orders, increased speed. Soon the infantry had been left well behind.

Close at hand was the bridge across the Blue Krantz River, and Winston, seeing that Haldane and his men were now out of sight, ordered the engine driver to stop. The man obeyed, though he was loath to do so. He had seen safety ahead of him and he wanted to be at the other side of the bridge.

'Cross the bridge and wait for us on the other side,' he shouted to the driver. 'I'll go back and find Captain Haldane and the others. Something must have held them up.'

Almost before he stopped speaking, the engine started again. With its pathetic load it went forward over the bridge out of range of bullet and shell.

Winston, watching it go, turned and made back the way he had come. He knew he needn't have left the engine to return. After all, he was a noncombatant, a war correspondent. But he just couldn't abandon his friend Haldane and the others like that. He must see what had happened to them, help them to fight their way through if necessary.

CHAPTER TWELVE

PRISONER OF WAR

The line curved at this point. As he proceeded warily to the point where he had last seen Haldane and his men Winston kept a weather eye open.

Suddenly two men jumped down to the track just ahead of him from the steep bank. At first, seeing their dark clothes, he thought they were a couple of wounded platelayers who had been left behind; then he noticed their slouch hats, the rifles they carried.

Boers!

As one of the men raised his rifle and took aim Winston turned to run. Yet where could he go? If he ran back down the track toward the bridge, they would pick him off long before he got around the bend, and if he crouched against the side of the cutting, it would only be a matter of seconds before they came up with him.

There came the crack of the rifle. He felt the wind of the bullet as it went past his head. Turning to the bank, he began to scramble up it. Another shot. Once more the bullet missed.

A wire fence at the top of the bank confronted him. Diving at it, he scrambled through and flung himself down out of sight of the men on the line below. Already the strain of the last hour and a half was beginning to tell. His limbs were heavy. His heart was pounding. His breath was coming in painful gasps.

Looking round, he saw nearby a small stone cabin evidently for the use of platelayers. If he could reach it, he could perhaps hide, and the Boers might believe he had run to the rocky gorge of the river, some two hundred yards away.

Suddenly he decided that his chance of escape would be much brighter if he did try to reach the river. Once he had scrambled down the steep side of the gorge, he could plunge into the water and swim to the other side when the engine was waiting.

There was not a moment to waste. Getting to his feet, he made across the hillside toward the river.

Hearing a thunder of hoofs, he turned and looked over his shoulder. To his dismay he saw on the other side of the railway a horseman galloping furiously toward him. This man held a rifle in his right hand. Aware that Winston had seen him, he reined in his horse and shouted to him to halt.

The two faced each other across the railway

cutting. The rifle was now aimed at Winston, and the stern face and bleak eyes looking along the sights left the young Englishman in no doubt that if he acted foolishly, he would be shot down without mercy.

He remembered suddenly the Mauser pistol which, in spite of his noncombatant status, he had brought with him. If he could draw it, he might, with a bit of luck, kill this Boer before he could fire his rifle.

His hand crept to his belt—and groped in vain. Suddenly he remembered how, while working to clear the line for the return of the armored train, he had taken the pistol off. Now it was on the engine at the other side of the Blue Kratz River!

There was nothing for it but surrender. It was very galling. He had not even had the satisfaction of reaching Haldane and his men whom he had come to seek. If he had not let the engine go on, he might by this time have been on his way to the safety of Estcourt.

He raised his arms above his head and waited while the Boer, keeping his rifle trained on him, beckoned to him to cross the line to his side.

Winston obeyed, comforting himself with Napoleon's famous words: 'When one is alone and unarmed a surrender may be pardoned.'

But it was maddening for all that, and a few minutes later—after the Boer had fired his rifle across the river at the waiting engine with its pitiful load—he tramped by the horseman's side with a heavy heart along the track to where he had last seen Captain Haldane and his men.

He soon found that the others had already been made prisoner. Rain was falling as Winston and his captor made toward the Boer lines.

The young correspondent's gloomy thoughts were suddenly interrupted by a rather disturbing reflection. True enough he was no longer wearing his Mauser pistol, which might have led to him being shot out of hand, but he could feel, in each of his two breast pockets of his tunic, a clip of ammunition holding ten rounds.

He knew how dangerous to his own safety this ammunition might be. It as good as proved that he had set out with a weapon of some sort, which meant he could be court-martialed and shot.

Dropping back a little so that his bleak-eyed captor could not see what he was doing, he managed to remove one clip and drop it on the ground; but just as he had eased the other clip out of his pocket, the Boer turned and looked down at him.

'What have you got there?' he snapped.

'This!' Winston looked at the clip of ammunition with as much curiosity as if he had never seen it before. 'I just picked it up. Someone must have dropped it.'

124

The other examined it, then threw it away. Winston gave a soft sigh of relief. His tale had been believed.

Shortly afterward they reached the rest of the men who had been taken prisoner after the armored train fiasco. Hundreds of mounted Boers in dark clothes and big hats surrounded them and looked at them with interest. Many of them, because of the heavy rain, held umbrellas over their heads. The Englishmen examined their captors in their turn.

'Crikey! It's like fighting a blooming lot of churchwardens!' one of the Tommies muttered in disgust.

Little did Winston Churchill know on that day that the man who took him prisoner was none other than Louis Botha, later to be General Botha and one of his country's great statesmen. He was to learn this for the first time when three years later, the Boer generals came to England seeking assistance for their devastated country. Winston met him then without recognizing him; but when Botha recalled the incident, the young Englishman was delighted to renew the acquaintance begun in such strange circumstances.

For a long time after he had joined the other prisoners, Winston sat on the wet ground waiting his turn to be interviewed by the Boer intelligence officer.

His thoughts were bitter. He wouldn't have minded so much if his quixotic gesture in returning to seek his companions had been worthwhile. But it had been such a miserable anticlimax to be made prisoner before he could even contact the men he had gone back to help.

Now he would be put away in a prisoner-of-war camp for the duration of hostilities. His work for the *Morning Post* would never even begin.

What a fool he had been! What a fool!

But a few minutes later he had something else to worry about. For someone shouted his name. When he stood up, he was told to stand apart by himself.

What did this mean? he wondered uneasily. Could it be that, because he was in uniform, and had taken a very active part in rescuing the armored train even though he had not fired a shot, he was to be court-martialed? The wet day with darkness coming on, the bleak line of tents in which the interrogation of the prisoners was taking place, the apprehensive look which the Boers cast from time to time in the direction of Estcourt, where there was a fairly considerable force of British soldiers which might attack at any moment—these conditions meant that little time would be wasted over a man who might be a spy.

Soon enough, Winston knew, he would have to answer some awkward questions. He began to rehearse his replies. He must put on as good a show as possible. And if the worst came to worst

126

and he was put up against a wall and shot, he must try to die bravely.

But nothing like that happened to him. After a brief quarter of an hour's questioning he was told bluntly that he might join his companions. As he went from the tent he began to cherish a rather vague hope that because he was a noncombatant, the Boers might even let him go.

But this hope was short-lived. Soon a Boer officer came to him and told him that although they accepted his story that he was a journalist, he would still be treated as a prisoner of war.

'We don't catch the son of a lord every day,' the man said with a grin.

A short time later, still in driving rain, the sad procession of Britishers started off under escort for Elandslaagte, there to be put on a train and moved to Pretoria to a prison camp.

CHAPTER THIRTEEN

IN PRISON

Winston Churchill and his companions were three days on the journey to Pretoria, capital of the Boer Republic. The first fifty miles to Elandslaagte were made on foot. As they passed besieged Ladysmith they heard the sound of gunfire from British and Boer artillery.

From Elandslaagte they proceeded slowly by train northwestward. From time to time other prisoners were picked up. One of these was a trooper of the Imperial Light Horse called Brockie, who passed himself off to the Boers as an officer. He joined Churchill, Haldane, and another officer, an Irishman called Frankland. Because he spoke fluent Dutch and Kaffir, his companions did not expose his deception, deciding he might be a very useful man to have if ever a chance to escape presented itself.

Pretoria was reached on November 18, 1899. The noncommissioned officers and men on the train were taken off to a specially prepared 'cage' on the racecourse, while Winston Churchill and his companions were introduced to their new home, the State Model Schools. They found over fifty other officers already confined here, many having been prisoners since the disaster at Nicholson's Neck a month before. They were greeted eagerly and were soon passing on the latest news from 'the front.'

The State Model Schools stood in the middle of a quadrangle. On two sides was a ten-foot-high iron fence, on the others an iron grille. The guard consisted of men of the South African Republic Police known as Zarps; ten were constantly on sentry-go around the perimeter of the prison, which at night was brilliantly floodlit by electric lights on tall standards. The rest stood by for any emergency.

At first Winston tried to convince his captors that he was a noncombatant and was entitled by the rules of war to be released and sent back to his own lines. But the Boers would not agree to this. He had, they said, helped in the escape of the armored train. That was a warlike act and he would be held because of it.

After a time, the young man ceased to argue with his captors and began to concentrate on other matters. First it was escape. He was depressed horribly by confinement. Like an imprisoned tiger, he paced up and down the quarters he shared with Haldane and Frankland until he almost drove them mad with irritation.

He refused to play cards or to take part in any of the amusements which his companions invented to while away the time.

Escape! Escape! That was what they must do. He had no time for games and such nonsense when there were so many plans to make.

But soon another idea presented itself to his ingenious mind. Watching the sentries day by day, and memorizing their habits and their routine, it occurred to him that if he and his companions could overpower their guards, they could sally out into Pretoria, release the two thousand soldiers confined on the racecourse, and capture the capital of the Transvaal, thus striking at the very roots of Boer power to wage war.

At first the majority of officers thought he was

129

mad when he explained this plan, but when he and other enthusiasts pointed out that the few Zarps in the town were the only armed and able-bodied men available—all the young men were fighting with the Boer forces in Natal—he won several more adherents to his way of thinking.

The officers in the State Model Schools were allowed soldier servants from the prison on the racecourse, and these men passed on the news that their comrades were extremely discontented. They had, in fact, because their rations were short and their accommodations poor, threatened mutiny several times and had begun to worry their guards, who were so few in number.

'If we officers in the Schools could overpower our guard,' Winston said, 'and come up to take the racecourse guard in the rear as the men surged out of their camp, it would all be over in a matter of minutes.'

'And what then?' asked the skeptic.

'We could take the town over, for we should have all the arms necessary. Don't forget that though the Boers are good fighters out on the veldt, they've proved they're no good when they attack a strong position. Look at Ladysmith! Look at Mafeking! Look at Kimberley! Why, if we could hold on to Pretoria, the war might be over in a few days, for we'd control the railways and perhaps draw off most of the Boer army who'd hurry back to dislodge us. That would give General Buller just the chance he needs to end the war quickly!'

The plan was discussed day and night. It seemed to the young officers, all eager to escape, a magnificent chance to secure not only their freedom but lasting fame as well.

Careful watch was kept on the guards who did sentry-go around the perimeter. Their living quarters were in tents pitched to one side of the prison enclosure inside the fence.

Here, of the forty Zarps detailed for the duty, thirty were always sitting about during the day outside their tents cleaning their equipment, playing cards, smoking or lounging about, while ten were patrolling the fence. It seemed to the plotters that it would not be a very hazardous undertaking some night, after the nearest patrolling guard had been silenced, to slit the canvas of the tents and plunge in and overpower the sleepers within. The rest of the guard could then be tackled, and it seemed very likely that they would not hold out long against a force of determined young British officers three times their number, armed with their comrades' rifles.

Within a matter of minutes the State Model Schools would change hands and the captors become captives.

Winston was one of the strongest advocates of this hazardous plan.

'War demands the taking of risks,' he told the others. 'If we act to a concerted plan, all will be well. The more audacious we are the likelier we are to succeed. And think of the prize—the subjugation of the enemy's capital!'

When it was found that the cables which lit the floods around the prison by night passed through the prisoners' quarters, success seemed even surer. For one of the British officers, who had been an electrician in civilian life, said it would be a simple matter to plunge the whole prison into darkness. He proved his boast that night by disconnecting a cable. In the resulting confusion the sentries ran about in utter bewilderment, and Winston and his friends realized how easy it would be to waylay them in the dark and deal with them separately.

Accordingly, all their plans made, the committee charged with organizing the escape decided to seek the approval of the senior British officers in camp, who so far had been kept in ignorance. To their consternation their elaborately worked out scheme was turned down flat.

'It's much too dangerous an undertaking,' the senior officer said brusquely. 'You've no right to throw your lives away in such a madcap scheme.'

Winston and his friends argued, but all in vain. Yet so mercurial was their temperament that it was not very long before they were all busy making plans for individual breaks for freedom.

Beyond the eastern fence of the State Model Schools was a pleasant villa surrounded by a big garden. All the British officers who had ideas of escaping from their prison realized that their only chance lay in dropping over the high fence into this garden and slipping from it on to the road beyond.

The eastern fence had one big advantage over the other three barriers. Whereas the latter were brilliantly lighted after darkness by floodlamps, the eastern wall was in shadow. If therefore the latrines against this fence were entered, there was a good chance of a determined man jumping up, hooking his fingers over the top of the fence, and pulling himself up and over when the nearest guards had their backs turned.

Once in the darkness of the garden at the other side the escaper would them only have to watch his chance, slip out into the road, and walk boldly away through the town to the outskirts and the open country beyond.

Winston talked things over with Captain Haldane and the trooper who was masquerading as an officer, Brockie. Haldane and Brockie were not too keen on having Winston as a companion. They both knew that he was excitable. They felt that perhaps in a tight corner where tact and care were needed, he would spoil their chances by some rash act. But Winston talked them into agreeing to take him with them, and perhaps their decision was

133

swayed by Haldane feeling responsible for Winston's imprisonment, he having pressed him to go with him on the ill-fated armored train a month before.

On December 11, Winston and his two companions, accompanied by several friends, made for the latrine against the eastern wall. The sentries watched them enter with little interest. The crux of the plan, of course, depended on the guards failing to count those who later came out.

Winston and his friends intended to wait for a while, then when the sentries had their backs turned, make the attempt to reach the garden beyond the fence.

But everything went wrong. After the last officer had sauntered out and back across the enclosure to the dormitory building, the sentries took up their positions so that it was certain that they would see anyone's head which appeared even for a moment above the fence.

After a long wait Haldane decided it would be wisest to abandon the attempt that night, even though Winston wanted to risk it. Brockie supported Haldane and that was that! Disgruntled, Winston followed the others back to the building he had quitted an hour before with such hope.

But he was determined that he would escape. The following night, after Haldane and Brockie had again made another unsuccessful attempt to climb the iron fence, Winston went over to the latrine on his own. Through a slit in the metal wall he watched the two sentries. For a long time they seemed to stand waiting almost as if they expected at any moment to see him begin to climb over the fence.

Then suddenly, as if at a signal, one turned away and crossed to his companion's side. Both men, as if obeying Winston's will, turned their backs on him.

This was his chance. Standing on a ledge the young man sprang for the top of the fence, hung on desperately, then drew himself up. At first it seemed as if he would never be able to pull himself clear. He was also afraid that his scrabbling boots would kick the iron fence with a sound that would bring the sentries running.

Then with a last desperate heave he found himself lying along the top of the fence. He glanced across toward the sentries and saw, to his relief, that they were still laughing and talking together, their backs turned to him.

Now he had only to let himself down over the other side and he would be free.

He started to lower himself. Something pulled him up with a jerk. To his consternaton he realized that his waistcoat had caught in the ornamental metalwork at the top of the fence.

Desperately he fought to free himself. Again he glanced towards the sentries. Surely they would turn and see him. His luck just couldn't last any longer.

One of them was lighting a cigarette. Winston saw the glow of the match on the inside of his hands. It was an impression he was to carry with him for the rest of his life.

A couple of seconds later he was free and had dropped down to the garden below. There were some thick bushes and he hid among them to await Haldane and Brockie, who intended to make another attempt later.

To his consternation the garden seemed to be full of men. Once someone came to within a few feet of him, peering into the bushes as if searching for him, but after half a minute or so he went away.

Winston grew more and more impatient as the minutes passed. What were Haldane and Brockie doing? Surely they should have joined him by now.

Then after an hour he heard voices at the other side of the fence. Two officers were walking about inside the compound. They appeared to be jabbering in Latin, though once Winston caught his own name.

He coughed, and immediately a voice close at hand said, 'They can't manage it tonight. The sentry suspects. It's all up. You'd better try to get back.'

Winston was aghast. Why on earth hadn't Haldane made the effort instead of giving up so tamely? The whole success of this attempt at escape depended on the food, the maps, and compasses which Haldane had in his pocket. And Brockie, too, was an essential part of the plan. He spoke Dutch and Kaffir. How would it be possible for one man who didn't know a word of the native languages to get food and ask directions?

Yet Winston, in spite of these depressing thoughts, had no intention of returning. For one thing he doubted his ability to climb back over the fence, and for another he might never have such a chance of escape as this again.

No! he would go on. If he was captured later, he would at least have had a run for his money. It would break the monotony of captivity which he had now endured for a month.

Whispering his decision to those at the other side of the fence, he put on his hat, which he had carried so far in the pocket of the brown flannel suit he wore, and crossed the garden toward the gate leading into the road.

Outside he knew there was a sentry. There was only one thing to do. He must put on a bold front and pretend he had come from the house.

Head up, he strode past the man, who gave him only a casual glance. Turning left he set off up the road. He longed to break into a run, but knew that if he did he would be lost.

But there was no following shout. With rising spirits he turned a corner. He had escaped. He was at large in Pretoria.

CHAPTER FOURTEEN

A FUGITIVE

It was still quite early and the streets of the town were filled with elderly burghers and their wives and families. Winston strode boldly along. He knew that his best course was to appear quite fearless. If he crept furtively through back streets, it was almost certain that he would be seen and questioned.

His one fear was that his youth might attract attention. For there were hardly any young men left in Pretoria by this time. They were all away fighting the British in Natal.

To his relief no one gave him a second glance, and soon he was away from the busy main streets, out in the suburbs. Half an hour after escaping from the prison camp he was leaning against the parapet of a small bridge which crossed a stream, considering what he should do next.

He was three hundred miles from the safety of Portuguese East Africa with, on all sides, his enemies and a virtually trackless countryside. It was certain that by morning every Boer for miles around Pretoria would be searching for him. The few roads would be blocked; the railways guarded; every household warned that to succor him would mean death.

Yet he had some advantages on his side. He was young and strong; he had a few slabs of chocolate in his pocket; in his notecase was seventy-five pounds, which was enough to bribe quite a lot of people to help him. If he could avoid his enemies long enough and if his strength held out, there was no reason why with a little luck he shouldn't win through. At any rate, he had a sporting chance.

Greatly cheered he looked round. In the sky Orion gleamed brightly. He remembered another time, only a year before, when this same star had guided him safely to the banks of the Nile when he was lost in the desert. Well, Orion should be his guide again.

He struck off across country. He must find the railway. His greatest chance of success lay in scrambling aboard some moving train which was heading toward Lourenço Marques in Portuguese territory. He would have to risk a search. At any rate, it would be harder to find him concealed in a truck than it would be at large in the countryside.

To his delight he very soon struck the railway. Though it ran north when his way was east, he decided that it must be the line he sought.

He followed the gleaming rails, keeping a keen eye open for any Boer pickets. Once or twice he found guards placed on bridges, and at such times he made a wide detour to avoid them, scrambling across valleys and wading through streams.

But always he came up to the line again. For now he was looking anxiously for a train to bear him on his way. Already he was tiring, for the going was rough and the constant need to keep alert was a strain.

If he could jump aboard a train he could lie hidden and hope that when he had to get down to the track again, he would be a great deal nearer his objective than he was now.

After a couple of hours he saw the lights of a station ahead. Giving it a wide berth, he lay in a ditch by the track, waiting. He decided that if a train came along it would almost certainly stop at the station. That would mean, when once more it started, it would not have got up much speed as it passed his hiding place.

An hour passed. Winston grew impatient. The night was cold. He thought a trifle wistfully of his warm bed back at the State Model Schools. Then he smiled wryly. Why, every man back there, safe and warm in his bed, would give his right hand to be in his shoes at this moment, free and heading for safety!

Suddenly his attention was attracted by a light flashing in the distance. A train was approaching, its headlights stabbing the darkness.

Soon it came into sight, slowing for the

station. From where he lay the young man could hear the shrill hiss of escaping steam.

He waited tensely. Would the train never start? It took all his will power not to leave the ditch and board it while it was at a standstill.

Then it moved. Slowly at first, then with increasing swiftness, it came toward him. He left the ditch and stood waiting. He was alarmed at the monster's speed. He had never expected it to accelerate so quickly.

He saw the engine driver in his cab, a black figure against the glow from the furnace. He seemed to be staring out at the track, and Winston wondered if he had been seen.

Then the engine was past, and he was jumping for a passing truck, running alongside as he desperately strove to catch hold of anything that would haul him aboard.

As the line of trucks slid past, their pace increasing with every second, he began to despair. If this train went on without him, no other might appear before daylight. And that meant that he would have to lie up all day in what appeared to be a very sparsely wooded countryside. It was almost certain he would be seen and arrested.

Something swung above him—a rope, a chain?—and he clutched wildly at it. Hanging on, he ran with giant strides alongside the trucks, then swung himself up, to arrive precariously on the couplings between two trucks. After a desperate struggle he seated himself and looked around.

The train was now moving at a fast speed eastward. Winston raised himself and examined the truck behind which he was perched.

This was filled with empty sacks. Looking beyond this truck he could see the engine in the distance. It was obvious that he had joined a goods train and that except for the engine driver and his mate and perhaps a guard at the back, no one was likely to interfere with him.

As he clambered into the truck and snuggled down under the sacks he wondered if the driver had seen him. Well, what was the good of meeting trouble halfway? If the train stopped at the next station, he must be alert in case the trucks were searched. It was more likely, he decided as he lay comfortably among the sacks, that the driver hadn't seen him at all and that he would be left undisturbed until the end of the trip.

He noticed that there was coal dust at the bottom of the truck and on the sacks into which he was burrowed. He decided that he had boarded a coal train which was returning to the colliery for another load.

Soon the motion of the train lulled him to slumber. He slept uneasily and wakened while it was still dark.

He decided he had better leave the train while there was still time to find a hiding place which would shelter him during the daylight. Besides, he was parched with thirst, which meant hunting for a pool before first light.

Looking cautiously up the train toward the engine, he climbed over the edge of the truck and back to the couplings. The locomotive was moving at a fast speed. Seeing the first glimmer of dawn in the sky, Winston knew he must lose no time or he would be seen, either by someone on the train or perhaps by a farmer in a field near the line.

Drawing a deep breath and praying that he would land on something soft, he sprang outward. Though he sprawled heavily in a ditch, he was relieved to find, when he sat up, that he had not broken any bones.

He was in the middle of a wide valley. Low hills were outlined blackly against the growing dawn.

Soon he found a clear pool and drank thirstily. As the sky lightened he examined the railway line he had left. To his intense relief he saw that it was heading toward the sunrise. His long journey had started in the right direction after all. He must be full thirty or forty miles from Pretoria, thanks to the coal train.

Alarmed by the growing light, Winston looked around for some place where he could hide. The hills seemed to offer the best chance of sanctuary, and he started toward them. Soon he was entering a small grove of trees which covered the side of a deep ravine.

Here he was to remain for the next fourteen hours. Though he longed to move on while he was strong and not too exhausted, prudence warned him that if he left the cover of the trees, he would almost certainly be seen and questioned. He checked his impatience, therefore, stamping about to combat the coldness of the early part of the morning, lying in the deepest shade when the sun rose and the heat became overpowering.

He was not cheered by the sight of a huge vulture, which early spotted him and settled in a nearby tree to await developments.

From where he lay Winston could see down the long valley. Some three miles away was a little town, its tin roofs shining in the powerful sunshine. Here and there were farmsteads, and at the foot of the hill on which he lay hidden was a Kaffir kraal with its inhabitants cultivating the ground around their huts.

Winston, though ravenously hungry, contented himself with one of his slabs of chocolate. This added to the heat made him very thirsty. But the pool was out in the open and he dare not leave the wood because by the middle of the day there were quite a number of people—black and white—moving about, and he would almost certainly have been seen.

From where he lay the young man could see the railway line, and he observed with interest the several trains that passed in both directions. If there were as many trains by night as there were by day, he should have no difficulty when darkness fell in getting another lift on his way.

At last the interminable day drew to its close. As soon as the sun disappeared, Winston left his hiding place and made for the track. His plan was simple. He would wait on a steepish gradient, preferably near a curve, and would then mount the train, which would have been considerably slowed down. Because of the bend he would be able to climb aboard while the engine and the guard's van were hidden from view, the former having passed out of sight, the latter not having yet come into view.

He had been depressed and impatient during the day, but now that he was moving again and had slaked his thirst, he was quite cheerful. If he managed to move on another sixty or so miles tonight, he could lie up again the next day and repeat the process on the following night and the night after. In that way he would soon reach the Portuguese frontier and safety.

True, he would be hungry, for by that time the few slabs of chocolate and the handful of broken biscuits at the bottom of his pocket would have been consumed. But he would not die of starvation. Men had lived for many days without food. Provided he could find water to drink he would get through. And think of the meal he would have when he reached

Delagoa Bay!

These thoughts sustained him as he waited by the side of the track for a train. Away to his left the line disappeared round a gentle curve at a slightly higher level than it swept into sight a hundred yards below to the right.

Crouching behind a bush, he waited, patiently at first, then with growing impatience as the time passed. One hour, two hours, three hours crawled by. Surely a train must be due now! There had not been such a big gap between trains during the day.

A horrible thought occurred to him. Suppose the Boers had suspended all train movement during the night. It seemed very likely. The train he had caught on the previous night might have been an exception to the general rule.

When another hour had passed, he walked on along the line. If he stayed where he was any longer, daylight would find him no further on his journey. If he walked briskly forward, he could perhaps cover some twelve or so miles during the remaining hours of darkness.

But he soon realized how well guarded the railway was. At each bridge there were men, and many of the platelayers' huts he passed had lights. Then there were stations with villages clustered about them.

Soon he was leaving the line and making wide detours every half hour or so, pushing his way across bogs and swamps, wading through deep streams, forcing aside clinging brambles which tore at his clothes and scratched his face.

Soon all he wanted to do was lie down and sleep. But that was impossible. Dawn was not far off. If he was still out in the open when the sun rose, he would be spotted for a certainty.

As he approached yet another station he saw that three trains were standing in sidings. It was obvious that they had halted there for the night and that their crews were sleeping in the huts which surrounded the tin-roofed halt.

He went closer. Should he climb aboard one of the trains and lie there all night in the hope that in the morning he would be carried toward his destination? Yet suppose the train stopped unexpectedly and was unloaded. Discovery would then be certain.

If he could examine the trains, he might be able to see their destination. If, for instance, one had its goods consigned through to Lourenço Marques, it might be worth the risk to burrow under a tarpaulin and stay there indefinitely.

Slipping between two of the motionless trains, he began to examine the markings on the sides of the trucks. Suddenly he heard voices. Several men were coming along the platform toward him.

There was nothing for it but flight. Ducking under a truck, Winston made off across the veldt again.

This time he kept well away from the railway.

On the horizon he could see several bright lights which he took to be those of some important station. Away over to the left gleamed several fires, and he supposed them to belong to some Kaffir kraal.

He wondered if it might be worth his while to make toward them. After all, the Kaffirs hated the Boers, who were consistently cruel to them. They had, on the other hand, always shown themselves to be friendly toward the British.

Perhaps he could induce the members of some Kaffir household to hide him until the hue and cry had died away. He had money. He might be able to buy a pony and some food and thus start on his way again with a greater hope of success.

He walked on rapidly toward the Kaffir kraal, which he had believed to be about two miles from the railway. But after an hour the fires seemed just as far off as ever. However, his mind was made up and on he plodded, though he was weary to the point of exhaustion.

About three o'clock in the morning he approached a group of buildings. As he stood examining them, he knew for a certainty that they were not occupied by Kaffirs. They were, in fact, a group of houses set about the headstock of a coal pit. Against the sky the winding gear was plain to be seen; the fires came from the furnaces which worked the engines.

Going even closer, Winston saw that standing a little apart from the main cluster of buildings was a small stone house. Weak from lack of food, exhausted from his long trek, he looked at the house with longing. Inside would be shelter, warmth, food. Behind him lay the interminable cruel wastes of the Transvaal veldt.

Some instinct told him that he must go up to the house and knock on its door. After all, one of the things he had discussed with other officers in Pretoria before leaving was that near Middleburg there were several English engineers who had been allowed to stay in Boer territory because their skill was needed to keep the mines in good order.

It was more than likely, of course, that whoever opened the door would turn out to be a Boer, not an Englishman; but even if that happened he had his seventy-five pounds, and a Boer, especially if he was not in favor of the war his fellow countrymen were waging, might weaken when he saw a wad of notes waved under his nose.

Setting his jaw, his eyes gleaming with resolution in the light from the furnace fires, Winston Churchill strode across the space which separated him from the little house.

Raising his fist, he hammered on the door.

CHAPTER FIFTEEN

UNDERGROUND

At first there was silence, then as the young man again raised his fist a light sprang up on the first floor. A window was opened and a head looked out.

'Who is it?' a hoarse voice demanded in Dutch.

Winston's heart sank. He had hoped to hear an English voice. The man above must surely be a Boer.

But there was no backing out now.

'I've had an accident,' he called back. 'I need help.'

The window was closed. A moment later heavy steps sounded inside the house, then a bolt was drawn and the door opened.

A tall man with an overcoat thrown over his night attire looked out. The glow from the furnace fires fell on his long pale face with its dark mustache and anxious eyes.

'What do you want?' he asked, and this time the words were in English.

Winston, eager to get into the house and talk quietly with this man—who did not seem particularly hostile—began to pour out a story on the spur of the moment.

He said he was a Boer soldier returning to his commando by train. Fooling about with his companions, he had fallen on to the track. The train had gone on, and when he recovered consciousness, he found he had dislocated his shoulder.

The man regarded him in silence for a while, then throwing wide the door, invited him in. Winston was conscious of the revolver in the other's hand. He knew that if he made a false move he would be shot.

When he was standing in the dark passage, the man leaned past him, turned a handle, and threw open a door.

'Go in there,' he directed, and Winston did as he was ordered.

The man followed. A few seconds later he had lit the lamp on the table to reveal a small room which no doubt served as dining room and study. There was a table, a desk, and two or three chairs.

Laying his revolver on the table, the man examined his visitor keenly.

'Tell me more about this accident of yours,' he said, and Winston could see from his somber eyes that he had not been hoodwinked by the tale he had heard.

Shrugging, the young correspondent said, 'I think you may prefer the truth.'

The other nodded, and Winston hesitated no longer.

151

'I am Winston Churchill, war correspondent of the *Morning Post*,' he said. 'I was a prisoner of war in Pretoria but I escaped last night. Now I am hoping to reach the frontier.' He tapped his breast pocket. 'I can pay well for any assistance I am given.'

For some time the man did not speak. Winston eyed him anxiously. What was to happen now? Would the other pick up the revolver and order him into the cellar, and there lock him up until the Boers sent an escort to take him back to Pretoria? Or would he demand the money he now knew was his for the taking.

Suddenly the man got to his feet. Crossing to the door, he listened for a moment, then locked it. Turning, he held out his hand, his eyes shining with excitement.

'God must have guided you here,' he said feelingly. 'Any man but me would have given you up. The other Britishers here won't let you down, either.'

Winston sank into a chair. The relief at hearing these words was so great that all strength seemed to ebb from his limbs.

Only a moment before, he had believed that all was up, that in a matter of hours he would be returning to the prison compound. Now—now freedom was not a mirage any longer. It was becoming a very solid hope indeed.

His new-found friend now introduced himself as Mr. John Howard, manager of the Transvaal

Colleries.

'I became a naturalized burgher some years ago,' he said. 'When war broke out, the Boers seemed to think I would be more use looking after this colliery than as a soldier whose loyalty, to say the least of it, could hardly be relied on when fighting against his own countrymen. So with two or three others I've stayed on at the mine supervising the pumping out and seeing that everything is kept shipshape until production starts again after the war.'

He told his guest that besides him, there was a British secretary, an engine man from Lancashire, and two Scottish miners. All were British subjects and had not been taken into custody when they agreed to give their parole to observe strict neutrality in the struggle.

A disturbing thought struck Winston Churchill.

'But if you harbor me and the Boers find out, you'll be shot out of hand,' he said.

Howard shook his head with a smile.

'I can look after myself,' he said. 'As a matter of fact, I knew all about your escape. A field cornet came round this afternoon looking for you. There's a search going on all over the district at the present moment. It's a wonder you didn't stumble into a patrol coming here.'

'If you give me a few necessities—food, a pistol, perhaps a pony—I can make my own way to the coast,' Winston said. 'If I march by night and lie up by day, and keep away from the railway and towns, I should get through.'

But Howard shook his head.

'You'd be taken before morning,' he said. 'No! I have a better plan. But one thing I must beg of you, Mr. Churchill. Keep perfectly silent in here for the time being. There are two Dutch servant girls asleep in the house, and they'd give you away without a moment's thought, as it would naturally be their duty to do. There are Kaffirs employed about the mine, and though some of them prefer the British to the Boers, they're none of them to be trusted, especially if there is a reward at stake. And now I will get you some food, for you look to be starving.'

He left the room, locking the door after him. His guest, helping himself to whisky from a bottle on the table, rejoiced at the good fortune which had guided his feet to such a sanctuary.

Presently Mr. Howard returned with a well-laden tray. As Winston tucked into a leg of mutton his new friend said that he had already been in touch with the other Britishers at the time.

'They're as keen to help you as I am,' he said. 'We've talked it over and this is what we propose. Before daylight you must be hidden away in the mine. There you must stay until we can make arrangements for passing you over the Portuguese border.'

'But the Kaffirs! Won't they see me when I'm

154

in the mine?'

'No! We'll see to it that they won't go near you. You'll be safe enough so long as you stay put. No wandering about, now!' As Winston finished his meal his new friend said, 'One difficulty will be in keeping you fed. My cook is responsible for all the food I eat. She'll soon know when any is missing. I'll have to have a jolly good story to account for the disappearance of most of that leg of mutton by morning!'

He laughed, seeing the dismay on the young man's face.

'Oh, don't worry about it! I'll think something up. And now if you're ready, we'd better be off. The sooner you're underground the better. And don't worry too much. I think we'll manage to make you fairly comfortable in spite of your surroundings.'

It was still dark as Mr. Howard, first cautiously reconnoitering, signaled to Winston that all was clear. Leading the way across the yard, they presently came to an enclosure inside which stood the winding wheel that lowered the cage into the pit.

Here a stout man was introduced to Winston as the mine engineer, Mr. Dewsnap of Oldham. As they shook hands Mr. Dewsnap said in a broad Lancashire voice, 'When you go to Oldham again, lad, they'll all vote for you! Good luck!'

A moment later Winston was in the cage with

155

Mr. Howard. A lever was pulled and the cage fell swiftly into the darkness.

At the bottom of the shaft the two Scottish miners waited. They carried lanterns and a big bundle containing a mattress and blankets.

With Mr. Howard leading the way and the miners bringing up the rear, Winston walked along the twisting gallery. The lanterns threw their shadows before them, and as he plodded wearily along, for now his tiredness had returned, Winston felt the strangeness of his situation.

An hour before he had been in despair, ready almost to give up the unequal struggle. Now he was putting himself with high hopes completely in the hands of men he had not even known existed that morning.

Presently Mr. Howard turned into a small chamber seemingly hewn out of the solid rock. The air was cool and comparatively fresh.

'Here you can stay in perfect safety,' he said as the miners spread the mattress on the rocky floor and laid the blankets on top of it.

He produced a box of cigars, a bottle of whisky, and a couple of candles from his capacious pockets.

'These are from my private store, so my servants won't miss them,' he said. 'By tomorrow I'll have worked out a plan with these other chaps for feeding you.'

In the light of the candles he made up his bed.

Weary though he was, his mind was too active for sleep. He sat on the mattress and lit a cigar. A miracle had happened, yet he could hardly believe it.

Instead of capture and the humiliation of being hauled back to Pretoria, he was safe and sound in the care of friends. Soon he would be on his way to freedom with a wonderful tale to tell. Soon—soon he would be rejoining the army and taking his rightful place at the front, where he would once more report the clash of the armies. Of one thing he was certain. Whatever he did in future, he must avoid recapture. For if the Boers laid hands on him again, they would take very good care to see he never escaped them again. He must have made many enemies by his audacious escape from the State Model Schools. Next time the Boers might think it safer to shoot him out of hand.

On this reflection he laid down his cigar, blew out the light, and went to sleep.

When he wakened many hours later, he felt for the candles. To his consternation they had vanished. Believing they must have rolled out of reach, and not knowing what danger he might not land into if he started searching in the dark, he lay where he was, possessing himself in patience as best he could.

Hours later, or so it seemed, a faint light told him that someone was approaching. It was Mr. Howard.

'Why are you lying in the dark?' he asked, setting his lantern on the floor and regarding Winston with puzzled eyes.

'I can't find my candles anywhere!'

'Did you hide them under your mattress before you went to sleep?'

'No, should I have done?'

'You certainly should. The rats have got them. The whole mine is swarming with them.'

Mr. Howard told him that he had brought a chicken for his supper. This he had fetched from the house of an English doctor some twenty miles away.

'I daren't bring any food from my own house,' he said. 'I'm still not sure that my Dutch cook believed the story I told about a dog stealing the meat you ate last night.'

'I'm being an awful trouble to you! Wouldn't it be better if I went on, perhaps with a guide and a pony—'

'Nonsense! You're staying here. We'll get the food, never fear, even if I have to take double helpings myself at mealtimes and slip some of it off my plate into a bag when the servant's out of the room.

'Are the Boers still looking for me?'

'They certainly are. The government in Pretoria is furious you've escaped. They could have borne it better if you hadn't been so well known. The fact that round here there are quite a lot of Englishmen working the mines means they will comb the district pretty thoroughly. But don't worry! They'll not find you.'

He explained that one of the Scottish miners knew every inch of the mine. If the worst came to the worst and the Boers insisted on searching the pit, Mac would take Winston to a part of the workings which were practically underwater.

'Mac will dive with you under the water and stay with you until the hue and cry has died down,' Howard said.

'And the Kaffirs?'

'You needn't worry about them. They think this part of the mine is haunted, in any case. You wouldn't get them to come along here if you offered them a hundred pounds.'

Mr. Howard stayed a while until Winston had disposed of most of the chicken and several other tasty things he had brought with him, then, saying he had better return to the surface before he was missed, he handed over a fresh supply of candles, shook his guest's hand warmly, and departed.

Winston, tucking the candles away under the mattress, went off to sleep again. It seemed the only thing to do in the circumstances.

CHAPTER SIXTEEN

FREEDOM

He was awakened by a gentle tug at his blanket. He sat up with a start.

'Who is it?' he demanded, peering into the darkness.

There was a scurry of feet. Groping for one of his candles, he lit it.

The little rock chamber was empty, though he thought he saw for a moment a flash of white beyond the light, the glimmer of beady eyes.

Rats!

He examined his store of candles and found them intact. Evidently he had wakened in time to save them from the marauders.

He smiled to himself. He had far worse things to fear than rats. In any case they were very timid, for the whole time his candle was lit, they never ventured into the circle of its lights.

Once he dozed off, and when his candle guttered out, he was wakened as a rat scampered across his body. As soon as he lit up again, the tiny animals retreated into the darkness again. Evidently they were far more scared of him than he was of them!

The next day—December 14—was his third day of freedom. He was delighted to have a visit from the two Scottish miners, who brought him food and offered to show him something of the mine.

He was glad to stretch his legs in such pleasant company. As they walked along the galleries he was astonished to hear that the mine was only two hundred feet deep. He had thought it was at least half a mile.

Once Mac stopped and pointed up what appeared to be a chimney. Winston saw, as if through a telescope, a glimmer of daylight.

'It's a disused shaft,' the Scot told him.

They spent a couple of hours walking around the workings, and the young Englishman learnt a great deal about mining he had not known before. His questions were intelligent and to the point, and undoubtedly the Scottish miners, exiles in this foreign land, enjoyed airing their knowledge as much as he enjoyed being conducted around.

On this tour of inspection Winston saw large numbers of rats. 'They seemed rather nice little beasts, quite white, with dark eyes, which I was assured in the daylight were a bright pink,' he wrote later in *A Roving Commission*.

The next day Mr. Howard visited him to say that the hue and cry seemed to be dying away. The mining district had been thoroughly searched, and as no sign of the fugitive had been found, the Boers were driven to the conclusion that he was still hiding in Pretoria in the house of someone who sympathized with the British cause.

'They won't admit that you could possibly have got away from the town,' Howard said. 'As the search around here seems to have been called off, I see no reason why you shouldn't come up to the surface after dark and stretch your legs on the veldt.'

This plan appealed strongly to Winston. That evening, when Mr. Dewsnap had signaled that all was clear, the cage took him up to the top of the shaft again.

For the next couple of hours he strode across the open veldt, breathing in the exhilarating cold air which was so pleasant after the stuffy atmosphere of the coal mine. Mr. Howard accompanied him, and they talked eagerly of Winston's chances of escape.

'I've got the glimmerings of a plan,' Mr. Howard said, 'though I'd better not explain it in detail yet, for you might be disappointed if it didn't come off.'

Later, when Winston prepared to go back to his hideout in the mine, the manager told him that if things remained quiet, there seemed no reason why he shouldn't take up his quarters in the house next day in the room in which he and Mr. Howard had first talked together.

The following day Winston was smuggled out of the mine and into the inner office, where, hiding behind packing cases, he remained for

162

another three days, getting his exercise in the company of Mr. Howard or his assistant each night.

On December 16, Mr. Howard told him of plans he had made to get him to Portuguese East Africa.

The mine was linked to the main railway from Pretoria to Lourenço Marques by a single-track branch line. Along this line a Dutchman called Burgener was, on the 19th, sending a consignment of wool to Delagoa Bay.

Apparently Mr. Burgener was a friend of the British, who did a great deal of business with him.

'I've approached him,' Mr. Howard said, 'and he wants to help you escape. This is how he proposes to do it. His wool is packed in great bales and will fill two or three large trucks. The trucks will be loaded at the mine siding, and it will be easy to leave a small place in the middle of the bales where you can lie comfortably hidden. The bales will be covered over with a tarpaulin, and it is exceedingly unlikely that this will be removed at the frontier.'

Winston listened to all this with mixed feelings. For several days now he had regarded it as only a matter of time before he reached safety. This scheme of Mr. Howard's seemed chancy in the extreme. To lie helpless while the train was stopped at the frontier and searched was, in his opinion, asking for trouble.

He would have preferred by far to have been provided with a pony and left to find his own way to safety. In that way he could have controlled his own movements, hiding when danger threatened, moving on when the coast was clear.

But under Mr. Burgener's bales of wool he would be as helpless as a rat in a trap.

'I don't like it—' he muttered uneasily.

Mr. Howard strove to reassure him.

'Mr. Burgener's consignments are never examined,' he said. 'The odds against you being found hiding in the truck are very high.'

Presently he left the young man to think things over.

'Though you will have to make up your mind fairly soon,' he said. 'Mr. Burgener is risking a great deal and he won't expect you to be too choosy.'

Alone, Winston paced up and down, not knowing what decision to take. If he refused to go with the wool train, he might languish here at the mine for weeks, even months. And that would not be fair to John Howard who, if he was caught in his house, ran the risk of being shot for sheltering him.

Perhaps it would be a good idea if he slipped quietly away and on foot tried once more to reach Delagoa Bay. Then he remembered his last attempt to reach freedom with every man's hand against him, short of food, unable to speak the language. . . .

No! anything would be better than that. There was only one thing for it. He must accept this unknown Dutchman's generous offer and trust that the guards at the frontier would not examine too carefully the trucks containing Mr. Burgener's wool.

He told Howard his decision that evening, and the mine manager said he had chosen wisely.

The following day seemed never-ending to the young man crouched behind the packing cases in the mine office. He had a copy of *Kidnapped* and he read with mixed feelings the escape through the glens of David Balfour and Alan Breck.

Suddenly, when reading one of the most exciting passages, he heard the sounds of shots. Instantly he decided that the Boers had learned of his presence at the mine—maybe one of the Dutch servants had seen him after all—and that they had come to take him. The firing must mean that John Howard and his British assistants, knowing the game was up, were selling their lives dearly, knowing fully well that they would be shot in any case for helping an escaped prisoner-of-war.

What should he do? He had been told that in no circumstances must he leave his hiding place, yet ought he not to join Howard and the others in their hopeless struggle against overwhelming odds?

As he paced up and down, uncertain what to do, the firing ceased. Presently voices and laughter sounded, there was a clatter of hoofs, then footsteps came toward the office.

Winston, now once more behind the packing cases, peered out to see John Howard's grinning face regarding him.

'Don't look so scared,' he laughed. 'I've just had a visit from the Boer field cornet. No! he was not looking for you. He says you've already been arrested—yesterday at Waterval Boven. But as he didn't seem eager to go, I challenged him to a rifle match shooting at bottles. He won two pounds off me, so he has gone away delighted. He must have thought, if he stayed longer, I might win the money back!' He went on: 'It's all fixed for you to hide away in the wool after dark tonight.'

'What do I do?'

'Nothing. You simply follow me when I come.'

Soon after midnight Winston heard light footsteps approaching the door of the office. It was Howard carrying a lantern. Looking in, he beckoned to his guest, then without a word turned and led the way from the house to the siding where three large trucks stood partly loaded.

Howard avoided a party of Kaffirs who were lifting a huge bale into one of the trucks, and

166

made for the front of the train. Crossing the line, he looked at Winston, then nodded at the buffers of the first truck.

Winston did not hesitate. Jumping up, he peered into the truck and saw that a hole had been left between the wool bales sufficiently large for him to squeeze through. From this he was able to pass into the center of the truck by wriggling through a narrow tunnel dividing the bales. Here there was just room for him to lie stretched out or to sit up.

He heard a whisper. It was Howard standing alongside the truck.

'Are you all right?'

'Yes, thanks!'

'Then I'll be off. It won't do for me to be seen hanging about.'

'Good-bye. And a thousand thanks for all you have done for me. I'll always be grateful to you, Howard.'

But there was no reply. Already John Howard was making his way back to his house at the far side of the mine.

The next four hours passed with agonizing slowness, but at last Winston saw a gleam of daylight through a crack in the side of the wooden truck. Soon he heard the sound of an approaching engine, and the chink-chink of buffers as it gently collided with the trucks and was coupled to them.

As the train moved away from the mine

Winston examined the food with which the truck had been provisioned. There were two roast chickens, some slices of meat, a loaf of bread, a melon, and three bottles of cold tea. There was also a loaded revolver, though in the young man's opinion that was a doubtful blessing. If he was found armed, his fate might be worse than if he had nothing with which to defend himself.

The tunnel between the bales enabled him to move freely about the truck, and he spent much of his time peering through cracks at the passing scene. He had studied a map in Howard's office and knew the names of the various stations by heart. There were eleven between the mine and the frontier, the last being Komati Poort, where he most dreaded a search before the train passed into Portuguese territory.

At the first station, Witbank, there was a great deal of delay and shunting until, three hours after arrival, a main-line train came along and took the three trucks in tow. Soon they were off at a faster and much more satisfactory pace.

Winston's spirits rose as all day long the train ran swiftly across the veldt. Howard had told him that he should reach Lourenço Marques in about sixteen hours, but he knew well enough that it was impossible in wartime to say how long a journey might take. If they were held up in a siding, they might stand there for days.

That night they spent in Waterval Boven

station, half the distance to the frontier behind them. Winston, his eyes heavy with sleep, hesitated about closing them. Suppose, while they were at rest in the station, he snored. How ignominious it would be to be dragged out by some Kaffir, who, passing along the platform, heard him.

Yet in spite of this fear he fell into a deep sleep. He was awakened the following morning as the train jerked into motion again.

Once more the train rattled through the enemy countryside. Late in the afternoon they came to a halt in Komati Poort on the frontier.

Winston held his breath, hearing the shouts of men as they walked down the length of the train. Had a search begun already? Peering through a chink, he saw several armed Boers near at hand.

He decided that if a search of his truck was made he would ensure that he was not easily found. He therefore retreated to the very far end of his hiding place, laid himself on the floor, and pulled a piece of sacking over his body.

Then he lay, hardly breathing, to await developments.

Several hours passed. People walked up and down the platform, and on more than one occasion he was sure that men were scrambling about the trucks. But the tarpaulin over his head was not removed, and as far as he could tell, his truck had been left strictly alone.

Soon darknes fell. The agony of a long night wracked with anxiety lay before him. Once again he was afraid to sleep lest he snore and give himself away. But sleep would not be denied. With armed Dutchmen all around him he slept as soundly as a baby.

The train was still standing in the station when he awoke. A horrible thought came to him. Perhaps the search was so thorough that it was taking much longer than had been expected. Maybe, as his truck was right at the end of the train, the Boers had not yet reached it!

But suddenly, soon after eleven o'clock, sounds of coupling up reached him, then with a jerk the train moved forward again.

If his calculations were right, and the station in which he had spent the night really was Komati Poort, he was now passing into Portuguese territory.

He had done it! He was free!

But he restrained his excitement. It would be fatal to appear from under his tarpaulin if the train was still short of the frontier. How ignominious it would be, after the perils he had gone through, to be arrested and hauled off into captivity again just because he was lacking in patience.

Some minutes later the train drew up once more. This time Winston put his eye to a crack and peered out. His face lit up. He could hardly restrain a shout of delight.

For a few yards away was a sallow-faced individual in the uniform of a Portuguese official. On a board above his head was painted a name—Resana Garcia—the first station inside Portuguese territory.

Still he did not reveal himself. Komati Poort was still too near for him to take any risks. As he had come all this way, he would be patient for a little while longer.

But when the train started again and headed toward the sea, he climbed out from under the tarpaulin. Sitting in full view, he shouted and sang, even fired his revolver, in an excess of youthful exuberance.

Late that afternoon the train ran into a goods yard outside Lourenço Marques. As a gang of Kaffirs advanced to unload it, he slipped from his truck on the blind side and mingled with the people in the yard. His unkempt appearance gave the impression that he was a loafer who had been hanging about hoping to pick up a job.

Presently he reached the gate and made into the street. Outside the Dutchman, Burgener, was standing. When he saw the young Englishman, he nodded, then turned and walked off into the town.

Winston followed. Howard had arranged for Burgener to lead him to the British consulate, knowing that if he started wandering about Lourenço Marques alone, unable to speak the language, the odds were that he would finish up in the local police station. There some pro-Boer sympathizers might ship him back to the Transvaal before the British consul was even aware he had arrived.

Soon the Dutchman stopped and nodded at a building on the other side of the street. Winston followed the direction of his glance. His heart gave a leap of joy.

For floating above the house opposite was a Union Jack.

A moment later Burgener, with a casual nod, had disappeared. Winston approached the front door of the consulate.

His dirty, unshaven condition did not recommend him to the man who answered his ring. Winston asked to see the consul.

'Be off with you,' the fellow cried. 'The consul cannot see you today. Come back at nine o'clock tomorrow, if you want anything.'

'But I must see him! It's important! I've just escaped from the Boers.'

But the man was not convinced and again tried to shut the door in the visitor's face. Winston raised his voice.

'I'm going to see the consul if I've to camp out on the steps all night!' he cried. 'Tell him Winston Churchill is here.'

Before the man could take in this staggering information—for, like everybody else, he had read the newspapers, which for days had been

172

full of Winston's escape—a voice sounded from an upstairs window.

'Who did you say you were?' it asked incredulously.

Winston repeated his name. The window slammed. A moment later the owner of his voice was at the door. He grasped Winston's hand.

'Welcome, Mr. Churchill, welcome!' he cried in great excitement. 'I am the consul. Come inside. You must be tired and hungry.'

Within an hour Winston had had a hot bath, an excellent dinner, and had read the newspapers which gave such graphic accounts of his escape. He was interested to see in several of the reports that he had already been arrested in several places. One newspaper even went so far as to say he would probably be tried and shot when his captors returned him to Pretoria.

'There's a reward of twenty-five pounds out for you,' the consul said with a smile and pointed to a reproduction of a poster that had been distributed widely throughout the Transvaal.

Winston learned from the newspapers that since he had climbed the wall of his prison, the British army had been badly beaten, with big casualties, in three great battles: at Stormberg, Magersfontein, and Colenso.

England was staggered by these reverses. The war that had seemed likely to last only a few weeks now seemed doomed to go on indefinitely.

Winston decided that the sooner he rejoined the army the better. In this he was backed up by the consul, who knew that though Lourenço Marques was Portuguese, the town was full of Boers and Boer sympathizers who might try to hold Winston and return him to the Transvaal.

'The weekly steamer is leaving for Durban this evening,' the consul said. 'I'll book you a passage.'

'That suits me perfectly,' Winston replied.

Some time later, when they were at dinner, the murmur of voices came from the garden outside. The consul crossed to the window and glanced through.

'It looks as if we're in for a demonstration,' he muttered uneasily.

Winston joined him. Moving about in the garden were a large number of men.

'Do you think they are Boers?' he asked.

At that moment the door opened, and a servant came in.

'A gentleman wishes to speak to you, sir,' he said. 'He is an English gentleman.'

'Let him come in,' the consul said.

A moment later the caller entered. He was a British resident and he said that he with other Britishers had heard with delight of the arrival of Mr. Churchill. Because there was a danger that the Boers in the town might make an attempt to recapture the young war correspondent, he and his friends had armed themselves and intended to guard him until he left Lourenço Marques for Durban.

Winston thanked him cordially. Later, under the escort of these patriotic gentlemen, with many scowling Boers looking on, he marched safely through the streets to the quay, where the steamship *Induna* waited.

At ten o'clock that night he was at sea.

CHAPTER SEVENTEEN

BACK TO THE FRONT

Winston Churchill was received in Durban with flags, bands, and cheering crowds. All the dignitaries of the town came aboard the *Induna* to congratulate him on his escape.

Later he was carried on the shoulders of the wildly excited mob to the Town Hall, where he made a speech which was received with great enthusiasm.

Every household in Durban wished to entertain him. But his one desire was to be back with the army. After he had read the many telegrams that had flowed in from all over the world, he left for the firing line.

That night he slept in the very platelayer's hut near which, little more than a month before, he had been taken prisoner.

The following day—which was Christmas Eve—many friends who had heard of his return came across country to celebrate with him the great Christian festival and to hear from his own lips something of his adventures.

In the New Year, newspapers began to reach him which contained accounts of his escape. The majority of the press treated him as a hero. He read that when news of his escape into Portuguese East Africa had reached London, there had been scenes of wild jubilation. After the dreadful news of the last few weeks his escape had been a much-needed tonic.

The Boers might have beaten the British in three battles, but they had not been able to hold a young war correspondent who had slipped through three hundred miles of their territory under the noses of thousands of searchers.

It was the very story which appealed to the Britisher, who was always on the side of the underdog.

But all the newspapers did not praise him. The *Daily News* (now extinct) said: 'Mr. Churchill's escape is not regarded in military circles as either a brilliant or honorable exploit. He was captured as a combatant, and of course placed under the same parole as the officers taken prisoner. He had, however, chosen to disregard an honorable undertaking, and it would not be surprising if the Pretoria authorities adopted more strenuous measures to prevent such conduct. . . .'

This report infuriated Winston. He had been guarded at the State Model Schools by heavily armed men, so the question of parole had never risen. It had been his duty to escape. Whenever this charge was made in future, he always threatened to take legal action against his detractors for spreading slander.

He also saw several reports of how he had been taken prisoner after the armored train incident. Here again, though the majority praised him for his part in the affair, one or two newspapers and periodicals took another tone.

Truth, for instance, said: 'The train was upset and Mr. Churchill is described as having rallied the force by calling out "Be men! Be men!" But what can the officers have been doing who were in command of the detachment? Again, were the men showing signs of behaving otherwise than as men? Would officers in command on the battlefields permit a journalist to "rally" those who were under their orders?'

There were others in a like strain, but on the whole the journalists had written of Winston's exploits as something worthy of the highest praise.

Soon after he had rejoined the British forces in the field, the *Morning Post* asked Winston to carry on as their correspondent once more, and soon he was sending a dispatch back to London which was greatly to excite military circles.

In it he said that Britain must face the fact that an individual Boer, mounted in suitable country, was worth three to five regular soldiers. He said there was work in Natal for a quarter of a million men.

'More irregular corps are wanted,' he wrote. 'Are the gentlemen of England all fox-hunting? Why not an English Light Horse?'

When this report appeared, a sarcastic editorial appeared in a London newspaper.

'We have received no confirmation of the statement that Lord Lansdowne has, pending the arrival of Lord Roberts, appointed Mr. Winston Churchill to command the troops in South Africa with General Sir Redvers Buller, V.C., as his Chief of Staff,' it read.

Some of the old generals and colonels in a London club cabled to Winston Churchill: 'Best friends here hope you will not continue making a further ass of yourself.'

But whatever the Old Guard thought about the young correspondent's opinion on the military situation, it was not long before ten thousand Imperial Yeomanry and gentleman volunteers were sent to reinforce the professional army, which before hostilities ceased had grown to a quarter of a million British soldiers, five times the size of the whole Boer army.

Winston was soon summoned to the presence

of the commander in chief, who was eager to hear at firsthand some of his experiences while a prisoner of the Boers.

Winston told General Buller all he could, including any information he had been able to pick up while peering through the chinks in the side of his truck on the way to Delagoa Bay.

At the end of the account Sir Redvers said, 'You have done very well. Is there anything we can do for you?'

Winston at once replied that he would like a commission in one of the irregular corps which were being raised.

General Buller frowned. 'You know what the government thinks about journalists who want the best of two worlds, eh?'

This was a reference to criticism that had been made in London about men like Winston Churchill who, while keeping their commission in the army, also contributed to newspapers at home on their experiences. A year before the War Office had ruled that no soldier could be a correspondent and no correspondent a soldier.

Winston replied that he could not give up his work for the *Morning Post,* for he was under contract. This set General Buller a poser, for he genuinely wanted to help young Churchill, whom he liked.

'I tell you what I'll do,' he said at length. 'You can have a commission in Colonel Byng's regiment. You will have to do as much as you can for both jobs, but'—his eyes twinkled— 'you'll get no pay for ours!'

This suited Winston perfectly, and he lost no time in getting into uniform again and joining the squadron of the South African Light Horse in which he was to serve as a lieutenant.

He soon christened them the Cockyollybirds, because of the long plume of *sakabulu* feathers in the large wide-awake hat. The regiment consisted of six squadrons and over seven hundred mounted men with a battery of galloping Colt machine guns. It had been raised in Cape Colony by Colonel Julian Byng, a captain in the Tenth Hussars, and he made Winston his assistant adjutant, allowing him to go wherever he wished when the regiment was not actually fighting.

The next weeks passed happily for the young lieutenant, riding over the veldt on patrol, sitting with his mess tin round the campfire in the soft darkness of the South African night, sleeping under a wagon in the moonlight. Most of the South African Light Horse were from Natal and Cape Colony, but there were also hard-bitten adventurers from all over the world who had come at the call of adventure to join in the fighting against the Boers.

Winston Churchill's first action with the Cockyollybirds came at Spion Kop late in January 1900.

This attempt to relieve the hard-pressed

garrison of Ladysmith, which had now been besieged for nearly three months and was in imminent danger of starvation, ended in disaster. With more daring leaders the British force might have swept to overwhelming success.

Buller's army, which earlier had been repulsed with heavy losses at Colenso, tried a flanking movement, basing its attack on Spion Kop mountain. At first all went well, and with 19,000 infantry, 3,000 cavalry, and 60 guns, the river Tulega was crossed about twenty-five miles upstream from Colenso.

The cavalry, among them the Cockyollybirds, were sent on a left-handed movement around the west side of the mountain, while the main force was drawn up with its right resting on the base of Spion Kop. There was little opposition from the Boers until the horsemen reached open ground north of the mountain. At this point an easy march offered to Ladysmith.

Here the Boers fell into an ambush. Two squadrons of British cavalry, galloping along the lower ground by the river, waited at the edge of a spoon-shaped hollow. It was early evening and the scene was very peaceful. Suddenly someone said, 'Here they come!' and looking across the depression, Winston saw the first of the Boers trot from the shelter of the trees as if unaware that there was an enemy within miles.

Soon about two hundred Boers were moving

across the hollow in pairs.

'Fire!'

The order rang out, loud and clear through the evening air, and the carbines poured a murderous fire into the astonished Boers below.

Instantly there was confusion. Men fell, horses reared and plunged, those still mounted either made for the cover of the trees or fired their rifles at the concealed British troops.

It was over in a few minutes. The Boers were in full flight, leaving many dead and wounded on the ground and some thirty prisoners in British hands.

Eager to exploit this little action—for scouts reported panic in the Boer lines toward Ladysmith—Winston and his companions were keen to push on over the open ground and make for the besieged town. But to their dismay an order came for them to withdraw to the main position, where the British troops on Spion Kop were now coming under a murderous shrapnel and rifle fire from concealed Boer guns and riflemen.

Winston, ever keen on military tactics, rode out with a companion to see what was happening on the top of the rocky mountain, which had a flat top about the size of Trafalgar Square.

Here two thousand British soldiers, on the night of January 23, had seized the summit. There was little cover, and when day dawned, the Boers brought up strong forces to keep them under constant fire. The British soldiers, cowering in their shallow trenches, soon suffered appalling casualties without being in a position to retaliate. Their general was killed in the first few hours and a Colonel Thorneycroft was put in command of all troops on top of the mountain.

Winston Churchill and his friend, leaving their horses at the foot of the mountain, climbed from one boulder to another up the steep hillside. Streams of wounded men constantly passed them on the way back to the hospital tents below.

Reaching the edge of the plateau, the two young cavalrymen looked aghast at the carnage before them. Rifle fire from Boer sharpshooters was constant while overhead shrapnel bursts sent hot slivers of steel in all directions. The shallow trenches dug by the British infantry were choked with dead and wounded.

'We'd better get back and report what we've seen,' Winston said, and turning about, they made their way down the mountain once more.

When they reached the headquarters of the Second Division, they asked to see General Warren, who gave them an anxious look.

'Your report is most valuable,' he said. 'I have had no report from the summit of the mountain for several hours.'

'They are in desperate need of reinforcements,' Winston said.

'They shall have them! We will send up fresh troops under cover of darkness, dig in all night, and hold the position with a much smaller force tomorrow.' He looked at the young officer. 'You shall go and tell all this to Colonel Thorneycroft, Churchill.'

'Very good, sir,' the young man said. 'But I would like the order in writing.'

'You shall have it!'

Some time later Winston was once more on the mountainside. Now darkness had fallen and there was little to be seen. He passed through the lines of a reserve battalion which by some oversight had been on the slope all day and had not been called on to aid Thorneycroft on the summit.

When he reached the plateau, much of the firing had died away. Picking his way across the stony ground, avoiding the groaning wounded and the tragically still shapes of men who would fight no more, he presently found Colonel Thorneycroft.

'Congratulations on your promotion, sir,' he said, handing over General Warren's note.

'Promotion!' Thorneycroft lifted a pair of exhausted eyes. He was plainly puzzled.

'You've been promoted brigadier-general, sir,' Winston said, having learned this from General Warren before he left.

'Precious lot of brigadier there'll be

184

tomorrow,' Thorneycroft grunted. 'I ordered a general retirement an hour ago.'

He glanced at the note the young man had handed to him.

'There is nothing definite in this,' he said impatiently. 'Reinforcements, indeed! There are too many men here already.'

'I am sure Sir Charles Warren meant you to hold on, sir,' Winston said in a worried voice.

But Thorneycroft shook his head.

'I've made up my mind,' he said. 'The retirement is already in progress. We have given up a lot of ground. We may be cut off at any moment.'

Unfortunately, there was no aide-de-camp or staff officer to advise him how serious a disobeyal of orders might prove. Winston, seeing the hunched tired shoulders of this man who had led his troops with bravery for over twenty-four hours, once even striking down a flag of truce which had been flown for a short time in the British lines and ordering the men to fight on, decided to stay by his side and help in any way he could.

In the darkness the long files of men made off in the darkness down the hill.

'Better six good battalions safely off the hill tonight than a bloody mop-up in the morning,' Thorneycroft said, watching them go.

At last he turned to his young companion.

'Our turn now, Churchill,' he said, and with a

last look round at the open space, which for so long had been an inferno of shot and shell, made off down the mountain.

Halfway down they met a long column of men armed with picks and shovels climbing to the summit.

'Who are you?' Thorneycroft demanded of an officer at their head, who held a shrouded lantern in his hand.

'I have a message for you, sir,' the man said and handed over the note.

'You read it,' Thorneycroft said and gave it to Winston.

'It says they are sending four hundred sappers and a fresh battalion, sir,' he said. 'You are to entrench yourselves strongly by morning.'

But Colonel Thorneycroft shook his head. He was not returning to the summit of Spion Kop for anybody. Waving his stick, he ordered the young sapper officer to turn his men back, then he strode on once more, Winston Churchill following at a short distance behind.

Winston was very upset. He knew that Thorneycroft had fought with exemplary bravery throughout the day. He had been left unsupported, without advice, when he needed it most. It was understandable that he should wish to save as much as possible from the disaster, after seeing so many of his men slaughtered under a merciless fire from which there was no shelter.

186

When they reached the base camp, Winston wakened General Warren.

'Colonel Thorneycroft is here, sir,' he said.

If he had expected an explosion, it did not come. Warren understood Thorneycroft's difficulty. He did not insist on his return to the top of Spion Kop.

The next day the Boers had reoccupied the mountain. They were shocked to see the piles of dead and wounded, and sent a message to the British lines that the wounded could be taken to hospital and the dead buried, a gesture that was accepted with gratitude.

Two days later, having suffered nearly two thousand casualties, the British army withdrew. Another attempt to relieve Ladysmith was made some days later, but again without success.

When this second action started, Winston was welcoming his young brother Jack Churchill, who had also secured a commission with the South African Light Horse. Together the brothers rode forward toward the enemy position on a ridge between the river and Ladysmith, and both thrilled at the sight of the heavy shells from a hundred guns bursting with great gouts of smoke.

But the artillery failed to shift the Boers, who hung on with great tenacity as the British infantry went in with the bayonet. The cavalry, when the infantry made little progress, were called off.

Two days after the attack started, the army fell back, leaving Ladysmith to sit behind its defenses and wonder how long the rats and horses on which its garrison now depended for sustenance, would last out.

CHAPTER EIGHTEEN

NEARLY A PRISONER AGAIN

There followed for Winston Churchill and his young nineteen-year-old brother days of story-book adventure. Healthy and strong, they mounted their horses each morning when the sun rose and went forth seeking trouble.

Galloping over the veldt, climbing the rocky hills, they exchanged shots with young men on the other side, rarely getting involved in anything more than a light skirmish. When they returned to camp, it was to eat a hearty meal, talk over the day's happenings with their friends, most of whom had had similar experiences, and sleep dreamlessly under the stars.

It was a state of affairs they would both have liked to see extended indefinitely.

On February 12 they set out side by side as usual to make a reconnaissance east of the railway line. Orders had been received to drive back the Boer patrols and pickets so that General Buller could personally inspect the terrain at that point.

For some hours they held a wooded slope in Boer territory, then, when the commander in chief had returned to the base camp, they followed in his wake. During the whole of the little action the Boers had kept up a lively rifle fire. When the British horsemen withdrew, they followed.

Winston, riding with his brother, looked back from time to time toward the position they had quitted. At first they had retired at a gallop, but now they were walking their horses leisurely up a slope. In a few moments they would be over the ridge and out of range of the Boers in the distance.

'You know, we are still much too near those fellows to be taking it so easily,' Winston said.

Before Jack could reply, a shot rang out, followed by a volley from three hundred rifles. Bullets flew like angry bees among the sauntering horsemen, and several men and horses were hit.

At once the long column spread out and galloped toward the safety of the ridge nearly two hundred yards away. Leaping from their horses, the cavalrymen threw themselves down in the long grass and returned the Boer fire.

Suddenly Winston, firing at the distant enemy, was conscious that his brother had put down his carbine and had wriggled out of the line.

'What's the matter?' he asked over his shoulder.

'I've been shot in the leg. It's nothing,' Jack replied, but his face was pale and he was obviously in pain.

Winston, crawling back to look for himself, saw that a bullet which must have passed between them had struck his brother in the calf.

A few moments later he was helping Jack back to an ambulance in the rear. He rode behind it as far as the field hospital.

This incident led to an amazing coincidence. During the last few months Lady Randolph Churchill had raised a fund and equipped a hospital ship. This with its complement of doctors and nurses had now reached Durban.

The first casualty to be brought aboard for treatment was her son Jack, and Lady Randolph received him as he was carried up the gangway on a stretcher. Later Winston took some leave and also visited the ship, where he was able to greet his mother after some six months of separation.

But on February 15 Winston was back with his regiment. The third attempt to relieve Ladysmith was about to be made.

Once again the Cockyollybirds were thrown out on the right flank to capture surrounding heights, and this they did with few casualties, driving the Boers from their fortified positions to stand looking triumphantly down on besieged Ladysmith some six miles away.

Had General Buller followed up this movement—for the Boers, fearing encirclement, had fallen back—Ladysmith might have been quickly relieved and at small cost. But for some reason the commander in chief withdrew his cavalry and committed his infantry to a frontal assault on strong hill positions still held by the Boers before Ladysmith.

Winston, who was constantly sending messages and cables back to the *Morning Post* about the fight to relieve the beleaguered garrison, rode to a commanding position to watch this attack, for he had been assured that this was an infantry responsibility and that the cavalry was not likely to be needed.

The attack was made by the Irish Brigade on a hill which is now known as Inniskilling Hill. It was late afternoon when the Inniskilling and Dublin Fusiliers began to climb the steep slope. Through his powerful glasses the young war correspondent could see the Boers lying in their concealed positions among the rocks and on the ridge.

The Irishmen moved slowly forward over bare ground which gave no cover at all. To the sharp-shooters up above they must have seemed like dummies provided for target practice.

When the foremost line fell writhing to the earth, the second took its place, and that also was swept away by the withering rifle fire. Soon the hillside in the red light of the sunset was littered with dead and dying men. The few who reached the summit were quickly dealt with.

Defeat was complete. Twelve hundred men attacked Inniskilling Hill. Of these 2 colonels, 3 majors, 20 other officers and 600 soldiers were lost.

General Buller now decided to do what he should have done in the first place; exploit the cavalry's earlier success on the Boer's left flank On February 27 the army delivered its final assault. By the end of the day most of the Boer positions had fallen. Inniskilling Hill, outflanked, was carried at the point of the bayonet.

Winston and his companions, seeing how the tide of the battle had turned, now mounted, meaning to ride after the fleeing Boers and cut them down. They were met at one of the crossings over the river by the commander in chief himself, who ordered them to return. There was to be no pursuit! Bitterly disappointed, the cavalrymen turned their mounts and trotted disconsolately back to camp.

But the next day they had their turn. Although the general still refused to allow any pursuit of the flying enemy—his reason was said to be that he believed in leaving well alone now victory was won!—the Cockyollybirds, with Winston Churchill in their midst, crossed the river with the cavalry brigade and reached the open plain which led to Ladysmith.

Toward evening two squadrons of the South African Light Horse rode into Ladysmith. Winston thrilled as they approached the outer barricades of the heroically held town to see two gaunt defenders rise from behind a barricade and wave a wild welcome.

As they made along a street, with cheering men and women coming out of the tin-roofed houses to greet them, they saw a faultlessly attired officer riding toward them.

It was Sir George White, who for so many weeks had refused to surrender to the overwhelming forces of Boers which had surrounded the town.

That night Winston dined with the head-quarters staff. A trek ox, the last in the town, was slain in honor of the occasion, and men who had fed on horseflesh for weeks had their first square meal since the siege began.

It was a great occasion. The victory brought to an end the long run of successes the Boers had enjoyed since the war started four months before.

With the retreat of the Boers from Natal, and the lull that must take place while the British army repaired railways and built up stores for the advance on Pretoria, Winston Churchill secured indefinite leave from the South African Light Horse and left for Cape Town.

It was his intention to get himself accredited as *Morning Post* correspondent to Lord Roberts' army. Lord Roberts had recently taken over as commander in chief, and, thanks to his energy and military skill, the earlier failures of British arms had been turned into the redounding successes of the relief of Kimberley and the capture of a Boer army at Paardeberg.

While Winston waited for his orders to come through, he spent a pleasant time in Cape Town, enjoying its social life and sending home reports of interviews he had had with prominent personages.

To his surprise he was not immediately summoned to Lord Roberts' headquarters. On inquiry he learned that the great man had taken exception to an article Winston had contributed to the *Morning Post* criticizing a sermon that had been preached to the troops before Spion Kop.

The young correspondent had expected something much more inspiring and had pointed out in his article that men about to fight—perhaps to die—needed to hear something other than a discourse about how the Israelites brought down the walls of Jericho.

Lord Roberts apparently had felt this criticism to be a reflection on the military chaplains' department, which came under his command, and decided to punish Winston by withholding the needed pass.

But Winston had strong friends at court, and one day the order came for him to proceed to Bloemfontein in the Orange Free State. Here, whenever he heard of the possibility of a fight, he would mount his horse and ride in the wake of the column detailed to make contact with the Boers.

Often he left one column and made across country to join another. This entailed long journeys alone in hostile territory. Sometimes he would arrive in time to join in a fight, then, when it was over, set off once more to find some other adventure, a description of which he could retail to his thousands of readers back in the homeland.

At last he decided to join his old friend General Brabazon, who had been put in command of the Imperial Yeomanry, lately arrived from England. No doubt he thought that public interest at home would be centered on these volunteers, the first to reach the field since war broke out.

When he overtook the British column on April 19, it was to find them preparing for battle. The Boer position before the town of Dewetsdorp lay ahead, and loud on the evening air came the rattle of musketry as the Boers reacted to British patrols pushed out ahead of the main force.

Due to the vacillation of the British general

and his advisers, the order to attack was delayed day after day, in spite of the fact that some 11,000 British troops had been assembled, backed by eighteen guns.

Brabazon was furious at what he considered to be feeble British leadership. When, for the third time, the attack was cancelled he gave vent to his anger. Perhaps to appease him and give the impatient cavalry something to do, the general ordered Brabazon to reconnoiter on the left flank.

Dewetsdorp was hidden from sight by a line of hills. A prominent feature was a peculiarly shaped kopje (hill), and near this, mounted or on foot, were about two hundred Boers.

When the Boers saw the advancing British cavalry they looked uncertainly at each other, not sure if they were about to be attacked or bypassed. After a while they started an outflanking movement, but so accurate was the fire of the cavalry that they broke off the engagement and disappeared behind the hill.

Almost immediately a new force of Boers appeared and made for the kopje on the British right flank. It was obvious that they meant to reach this, and using it as cover, pour a withering fire on to the British cavalry, who would be caught in the open.

A young officer called McNeill, in command of a squadron of scouts, galloped up to the general with a request.

'May we head them off, sir? I think we can just do it.'

Brabazon considered for a moment, then gave his consent.

Turning to Winston, who was near at hand, McNeill cried, 'Come with us, we'll give you a show now—first-class!'

The scouts looked at the war correspondent. Most of them knew that some time before he had promised to follow and report on their activities if the chance offered.

He looked across at the Boers. They were nearer to the kopje than the scouts; on the other hand, they had the slope to climb. It would be a fair race, and the winner would be able to command the open ground below, which would mean retreat and casualties for the unsuccessful.

Thinking of his duty toward the *Morning Post*, Winston threw himself on to his horse.

'Lead on!' he cried, and McNeill, giving an order, led the force of fifty scouts toward the kopje.

From the start both sides recognized it as a race. As the two forces converged, half a dozen Boers, better mounted than the others, drew away in a desperate attempt to reach the small hill and hold it until the main force came up.

'We'll never do it!' Winston muttered, but McNeill and his men showed no sign of pulling in their horses.

A few minutes later the British horsemen

197

reached a wire fence near the crest of the hill. Dismounting, they cut frantically at the thick strands, determined to gain the summit and hold it against the men climbing from the other side.

Suddenly, as they still worked, the head and shoulders of a dozen Boers showed on the skyline. Winston saw that one had a long drooping beard and a chocolate-colored coat, that another had a red scarf round his neck. As the scouts struggled desperately to cut through the wire the Boers raised their rifles and took aim.

'We're too late! Get back to the other kopje. Gallop!'

Then the rifles barked; bullets buzzed through the air. Winston, remembering how once before he had fallen into the hands of the Boers, did not waste any time. Putting his foot in the stirrup, he prepared to mount.

But the sudden rifle fire had startled his horse, which plunged wildly. As its rider tried to spring into the saddle the animal broke away and galloped madly down the slope.

Winston looked round. Already most of the scouts were some two hundred yards away, galloping to safety. He realized that he was alone, dismounted, and far from cover of any kind.

He felt for his pistol. This time at least he would not be hunted down, disarmed, and unable to defend himself.

He turned, and zig-zagging to spoil the aim of the marksmen on the ridge, ran down the side of the kopje.

Suddenly, as he ran, he saw one of the scouts coming up from the left. He was a tall man with a skull and crossbones badge.

'Give me a stirrup!' Winston yelled as he came near, and the man, though in real danger of being shot down for his pains, approached.

'Get up behind,' he said shortly.

Winston did not waste any time. In a moment he found himself seated on the sturdy horse behind its rider.

Bullets flew about them as they galloped away. Winston leaning over to grasp the horse's mane to steady himself, felt his hands soaked in a gush of blood. He knew then that the horse was hit and wondered how long it would be able to bear the weight of two men.

But the gallant beast galloped on until they were out of range. The trooper, as they slowed to a trot, said:

'Oh, my poor horse! Oh, my poor horse! He's been shot with an explosive bullet. The devils! But their hour will come. Oh, my poor horse!'

'Never mind,' Winston replied, 'you've saved my life.'

But the trooper only shook his head.

'Ah, but it's the horse I'm thinking about,' he said, and Winston realized, not for the first time, how greatly a man can become attached to the noble beast who carries him so well in the hour of danger and expects so little in return.

For his part in rescuing Winston Churchill on this occasion Trooper Roberts of the Montmorency's Scouts received the Distinguished Conduct Medal.

CHAPTER NINETEEN

A LAST ADVENTURE

The two young men cycled slowly along the street. Darkness was falling. A large number of anxious-faced people were either hurrying to and fro or standing in groups talking in low voices. Among them walked or rode armed Boer riflemen. There was an air of urgency abroad as if important events were in the making.

Only a few hours before, the order had been given by the Boer command to evacuate armed forces from Johannesburg. British troops under Lord Roberts were massing a few miles away.

'I told you no one would take any notice of us,' one of the cyclists said. He was a Frenchman and he spoke in his native tongue.

The other—Winston Churchill—looked cautiously round before replying in the same language.

'It is a little early to crow yet,' he muttered. 'We've to get to the other side of the city before we can get through to the commander in chief.'

He was in civilian clothes again after months in uniform. Only a few hours before, learning from the British general in charge of operations to the north of Johannesburg that much time was being lost by dispatching messengers on a circuitous route round the city from his command in army H.Q. at the other side, Winston had offered to take an urgent dispatch *through* the city rather than round it. He had heard from the young Frenchman, who was acting as his guide, that this would be possible.

He was warned before he left what would happen if he was caught. He was a commissioned officer disguised in plain clothes. There was only one possible sentence if he was brought before a court martial: death.

The two cyclists came to a steep street. Getting from their saddles, they started to push their cycles before them. They longed to hurry, for they were sure that the eyes of the passers-by were on them.

Suddenly they heard the measured pacing of a horseman ascending the hill behind them. The two young men exchanged glances.

'He's a long time passing us!' Winston said uneasily.

'Don't hurry! If he questions us, speak in French. He's not likely to understand.'

Presently the horseman came up with them. Winston met a pair of bleak eyes in a bearded face. The Boer had a rifle slung on his back, a pistol in his holster, and three bandoliers of cartridges at his waist.

After that first scrutiny the young man drew his eyes away from the other's curious gaze and concentrated on pushing his cycle along. For some time the horseman kept up with the two young men, neither increasing nor decreasing his pace.

Suddenly, as if making up his mind that they were harmless, he touched his horse with spurred boot and trotted ahead. As he did not look back or show any further sign of interest, Winston and his companion drew a sigh of relief.

But they remained on the alert. Though they were approaching the suburbs of the city, there were still likely to be Boer pickets watching for the approach of the British.

Soon however they were riding along at a good speed toward the houses on the outskirts. To their relief there were no Boers standing sentry, neither did they come up against any British scouts riding out ahead of the main force.

What they did see were a number of British soldiers sauntering down the roads, unarmed for the most part, their only desire to find food and drink in the city they believed to be empty.

'Where's the army?' Winston asked an approaching Tommy.

'Back there,' the man replied, jerking this thumb over his shoulder.

'You'd better be careful about wandering into the city just yet,' Winston said. 'There are plenty of armed Boers around still, and you're likely to be shot it you're careless.'

Winston and his friend cycled on, leaving the man looking after them in some consternation. The idea that he might be put against a wall and shot had evidently not suggested itself to him before.

Presently Winston was alighting outside the headquarters of Lord Roberts' leading division. An officer directed him to general headquarters, nearly ten miles to the south.

It was quite dark when he arrived. A surprised A.D.C. welcomed him.

'Who are you? What do you want?'

'I'm Winston Churchill. I have brought a dispatch for the C. in C. from General Hamilton.'

The officer looked at the young man as if he was unable to believe his ears, then, with a muttered request to wait, disappeared.

Winston waited impatiently. He was eager to telegraph his experiences in riding in plain clothes through Johannesburg while the Boers were still in possession to the *Morning Post*. Knowing he was on bad terms with Lord

Roberts because of the Spion Kop sermon, he would have preferred to hand over his dispatch and be gone about his business.

Presently the A.D.C. returned and asked Winston to follow him. Winston, as he obeyed, wondered uneasily what his reception would be.

Lord Roberts was dining with his headquarters staff. He greeted the young war correspondent with pleasure. There was no trace of animosity in his twinkling eyes.

'How did you get here?' he asked curiously.

'By the direct route, sir!'

'Through Jo'burg! But how could you? It is still occupied by the enemy.'

'The Boers are leaving, sir. The city is almost deserted,' Winston said.

Lord Roberts insisted on the young man joining the others at table. Winston was glad to do so. It was obvious that the C. in C. had forgiven him for his criticism in the *Morning Post*.

*   *   *

The campaign against the Boers seemed to be coming to an end, and that after only seven months of war. Pretoria, the last stronghold, fell four days after Johannesburg. Many of its Boer defenders withdrew north. For many weary months they were to harass the British in guerrilla actions, though this did not become obvious till later.

Winston, accompanied by his cousin, the Duke of Marlborough, rode early into Pretoria ahead of a column of British troops.

No outriders had gone ahead and so no plans had been made for their reception. For all they knew, a thousand armed Boers might be concealed in houses ready, when they came in sight, to pour a murderous fire into their ranks.

Winston and his cousin, along with other British officers, drew up at the closed gates of a railway crossing. A few moments later a long train steamed into view. This was drawn by two engines.

To the amazement of the watching British officers the carriage windows were crammed with armed Boers, who held rifles in their hands as if they were ready to use them at any moment.

It was a tense and terrifying situation. Had one of the Boers fired his rifle at the men who were coming to take over his beloved capital, there would undoubtedly have been a great loss of life on both sides.

But a hush fell as the train steamed slowly by. It was as if everybody—officers and men on the British side, bearded wild Boers on the other— had been stricken with paralysis and were unable to obey their instincts to shoot on sight.

Winston gave a sigh of relief as the train bearing its highly explosive cargo steamed slowly out of sight.

Ahead of the others he and Marlborough cantered into the city. They had one idea only in their minds: to reach the prison cage to which the officers with whom Winston had been imprisoned had been transferred from the State Model Schools.

Their one fear was that the man they had come to release had been carried off in the train which had left Pretoria but a few minutes before.

As they rounded a corner they saw a long tin building ahead. This was surrounded by a dense wire entanglement. Seeing this, Winston took off his hat and gave a loud cheer.

Marlborough touched his arm.

'Careful! There are still some guards,' he said.

Winston now examined the armed Boer guards who came out to see what all the excitement was about. He turned to his cousin.

'We've got to do something and do it at once,' he said.

Marlborough was equal to the occasion. Resplendent in the red tabs of a staff officer, he went quickly forward, informed the guard that Pretoria was being occupied by British troops, and ordered them to bring out the commandant.

When this gentleman appeared, Marlborough softened the blow of demanding the surrender of himself and his men by saying he would give a receipt for the guards' rifles.

A few moments later Winston was greeting the prisoners, who, realizing that the way to freedom had now been opened to them, rushed from the cage, seized the guards' rifles, and raised a homemade Union Jack on the flagstaff in place of the Transvaal banner.

A fortnight later, after taking part in the fight at Diamond Hill, which aimed at driving the Boers farther north away from Pretoria, Winston decided the time had come for him to return to England.

Though he suspected that the war in South Africa was far from over, there was little that he as a war correspondent could find to write about while the main British army was concerned in building up supplies and organizing the government in the annexed territories.

He knew that a General Election would soon be held at home, and he was determined to be there if a chance of being offered a constituency by the Conservative party presented itself. He therefore applied for his release from the army, and when this was granted, left by train for Cape Town.

His last adventure on South African soil happened on this journey. Like his first, it concerned a train. . . .

About a hundred miles south of Johannesburg the express in which he was traveling stopped with a sudden jerk. Winston climbed down to the line to investigate. As he did so a small shell landed on the embankment only a few yards away. Fortunately no one was hurt, though Winston staggered with the blast from the explosion.

From the windows of the long train hundreds of heads were peering. The express was crowded with troops from many regiments who were being sent south or home. There seemed, so far as the young war correspondent could see, no officer about.

Glancing ahead, he saw that a wooden bridge about a hundred yards down the line was in flames. The train had been about to pass over this when the driver of the engine had jammed on his brakes.

It was obvious that something must be done and done quickly, for the Boers had trained their gun on the track, and at any moment a shell might arrive and create havoc among the crowded carriages.

Remembering vividly his unhappy experience on the Ladysmith line eight months before, Winston decided that he must get the train back to the last halt they had passed—Kopjes Station—which was guarded by a British garrison armed with two 5-inch guns.

Running along the track to the engine, he jumped up to the footplate and ordered the driver to reverse and steam back instantly to safety. He was obeyed without question.

As the train started to move Winston saw, in a

dry watercourse under the burning bridge, several armed Boers.

Taking his pistol from his pocket, he blazed away at them as the train began to run back. Scattering, they made for safety without firing a shot in reply.

A few minutes later the train was safely back in Kopjes, where Winston learned that a fierce action was being fought at Honing Spruit farther down the line. An earlier train had been stopped and attacked by a large force of Boers supported by artillery.

The wooden bridge had been set on fire so that the soldiers on the following train should not go to the help of their hard-pressed comrades. However, though they suffered a loss of sixty or seventy men, the British troops in the ambushed train held out until the following day, when help reached them from the south.

Winston, who was eager to get to Cape Town, borrowed a horse. In the company of a troop of Australian Lancers he marched through the night.

A few days later he was aboard a liner headed for home.

CHAPTER TWENTY

'THE YOUNGEST MAN IN EUROPE'

On returning to England in the summer of 1900 Winston Churchill lectured in Leighton Buzzard on his experiences to a big audience gathered in the town hall. He was widely reported in the press on the following day.

It occurred to him that if the inhabitants of Leighton Buzzard were interested in hearing what had happened to him in South Africa, others might also welcome a lecture on the same subject.

He thereupon made arrangements to speak in all parts of the country, leaving the organizers of the tour in no doubt that he expected to be handsomely paid for his services as a lecturer.

For he knew that if he was elected to Parliament, he must have sufficient money behind him to keep him free from financial anxiety. M.P.s in those days were not paid a salary as they are today.

But before he could go ahead with this ambitious program, he was summoned to the Conservative central office. The government had decided on an immediate General Election while the voters were in a jubilant mood over the outcome of the war in South Africa.

Winston was offered the choice of several constituencies, but as he told the Oldham electors later, 'Oldham is the sort of place I want to represent in Parliament—a throbbing, pulsing, living place of work and working men.' And Oldham it was.

In those days British General Elections lasted for nearly six weeks. Polling Day at Oldham— October 1, 1900—was one of the earliest.

There was a certain element of showmanship in the young candidate's entry into the Lancashire mill town, whose inhabitants received him with great enthusiasm. Standing in a landau—the first of the procession of ten— Winston waved to the cheering crowds of enthusiastic operatives and mill girls.

Soon after his arrival in Oldham he described his escape from the Boers to an audience which filled every seat and aisle in the Theatre Royal. Knowing that Mr. John Howard and his friends who had aided him were now safely under the protection of British forces in the mining district where they lived, Winston for the first time told the story of how he had been hidden away in the pit.

'One of the men who stood by me was the engineer at the mine, a Mr. Dewsnap, whose name may be well known to you in Oldham,' he said.

Instantly there was a great shout from the audience, 'His wife's in the gallery!'

During the election campaign Winston urged that the Boer War was both just and necessary, that the Liberals had been wrong to oppose it and had even gone out of their way to hamper its prosecution.

When the votes were counted, one of the Liberal candidates headed the poll. Winston was in second place, having turned out his old opponent, Mr. Runciman.

Some confusion was caused in the country when a press agency sent out a report that Winston was at the bottom of the poll. Several of the national dailies, including the *Times*, printed this on the following day, having gone to press before the correction reached them.

The *Morning Post* belabored the anti-Boer War Liberal *Daily News*, which, thinking Winston defeated, had gleefully said: '...Mr. Churchill is at the bottom of the poll. This is an important result, for Oldham is an "index constituency."'

'It is somewhat pathetic to reflect,' said the Conservative *Morning Post* on the following day, 'that the jubilation of the *Daily News* cannot possibly have lasted more than twenty minutes.'

This was a reference to the eagerness of the *Daily News* to go to press with such a titbit when, if they had been patient for less than half an hour, a correction would have reached them, giving the true state of the poll.

So Winston Churchill achieved his ambition

and became a Member of Parliament. He was twenty-six years of age.

Before the election was over he had traveled to all parts of the country to support Conservative candidates, even appearing on the platform of Mr. Balfour, Leader of the House.

In the last weeks of 1900 he began his English lecture tour, and for five weeks spoke in all parts of the British Isles to enthusiastic audiences eager to hear his stories of adventure on the South African veldt. He was paid highly for these appearances. In Liverpool he received three hundred pounds when he addressed a huge audience in the Philharmonic Hall.

In the New Year he crossed the Atlantic and repeated his lectures in the United States and Canada. In New York his chairman was Mark Twain, who introduced him as 'the hero of five wars, the author of six books, and the future Prime Minister of Britain.'

His tour came to an end in February. In that time he had traveled many thousands of miles and had rarely passed a day, except Sundays, without addressing an audience.

But it had been well worthwhile. He found himself, when he took his seat in Parliament at the end of the month, with nearly ten thousand pounds in the bank.

His purpose had been achieved. He could now turn his talents to those of a legislator without having to worry too much about earning

213

his living.

It is interesting to see what was written about him at this time.

Julian Ralph, who visited Oldham to report the election for the *Daily Mail*, wrote:

'Winston Leonard Spencer Churchill is twenty-six years old, with the mind of a far older man and the vitality and enthusiasm of a far younger one. He is a well-built man above the average height, with very broad shoulders and the strong frame of his mother's people. But you have to forget and look away from his face in order to see his frame, for his face is of a highly nervous, wholly intellectual type. It does not need much to give it a strained and worn appearance, as if its youth was being permanently dried out of it by the intense force at work behind it. . . .

'But the next time you look at him he has sprung to his feet with the eagerness of a boy, his pale blue eyes are sparkling, his face is flushed, he is talking a vocal torrent and his hands and arms are driving home his words.

'Young Churchill is a genius. The species is not so broad or so overfamiliar that one can carelessly doubt of it.

'He finds it easier to vault out of a landau than to open the door when he is getting out to address his electors and win their unqualified admiration if he can.

'He talks with such ease that when he is

excited or very earnest his speech gushes from him faster than some mental buckets can catch it up.

'Like every man who has written a good deal and values form and balance and style, he arranges his ideas and composes his sentences in such a way that whatever he says reads as if it has been written.'

G. W. Steevens, famous war correspondent, wrote a sketch, which he titled 'The Youngest Man in Europe.' It is perhaps the finest assessment of Winston Churchill as a man of destiny that has ever appeared. It was written in 1899 shortly before the Boer War broke out, and is a fitting tribute with which to end this account of a great man's formative years.

'Winston Spencer Churchill,' wrote Steevens, 'is the youngest man in Europe. A gallery of young men's pictures could not possibly be complete without him, for there is no younger. In years he is a boy; in temperament he is also a boy; but in intention, in deliberate plan, purpose, adaptation of means to ends, he is already a man. In any other generation than this he would be a child. Anyone other than he, being a junior subaltern of Hussars, would be a boisterous, simple, fullhearted, empty-headed boy. But Churchill is a man, with ambitions fixed, with the steps toward their attainment clearly defined, with a precocious, almost uncanny judgment as to the efficacy of the means to the end.'

Later in the same sketch he continues:

'It was not possible that a man who had done so much so well at twenty-four would be altogether popular. Enemies he has probably none, but precocious success is not the way to win facile friendship—even when joined with modesty—and Winston Churchill is, outwardly, not modest. In the army especially, where the young are expected not to know better than their elders—or at least to keep their knowledge to themselves—his assurance has earned him many snubs. One general will delight in his lighthearted omniscience, the next, and the next will put a subaltern in his place. But Winston Churchill cannot be snubbed. His self-confidence bobs up irresistibly, though seniority and common sense and facts themselves conspire to force it down....

'He is ambitious and he is calculating; yet he is not cold and that saves him. His ambition is sanguine, runs in a torrent, and the calculation is hardly more than the rocks or the stumps which the torrent strikes for a second, yet which suffices to direct its course. It is not so much that he calculates how he is to make his career a success—how, frankly, he is to boom—but that he has a queer shrewd power of introspection, which tells him his gists and characters are such as will make him boom. He has not studied to make himself a demagogue, and he happens to

216

know it. . . .

'What he will become, who can say? At the rate he goes there will hardly be room for him in Parliament at thirty or in England at forty. It is a pace that cannot last, yet already he holds a vast lead of his contemporaries. Meanwhile he is a wonder—a boy with a man's ambitions and—more wonderful yet—a very mature man's self-appreciation—knowledge of his own powers and the extent to which each may be applied to set him forward on his road.'

HIGHLIGHTS OF
SIR WINSTON CHURCHILL'S LIFE

1874 Born Nov. 30 at Blenheim Palace, home of his grandfather, the Duke of Marlborough.

1888 Entered Harrow School.

1894 Passed out of Sandhurst.

1895 Gazetted to the 4th Hussars.

1895 Visited Cuba and came under fire for the first time.

1897 War correspondent with Malakand Field Force.

1898 Charge of the 21st Lancers at Omdurman.

1899 Defeated in By-Election at Oldham.

1899 (October) *Morning Post* war correspondent in South Africa covering Boer War.

1899 (November) Taken prisoner of war.

1899 (December) Reached Durban after escaping from Boers.

1900 (July) Returned to England.

1900 (October) Won By-Election at Oldham.

1901 (February) Entered House of Commons at age of twenty-six.

1908 President of Board of Trade in Liberal Administration.

1910–1911 Home Secretary.

1911–1915 First Lord of the Admiralty.

1915 Resigned from Government to go to France to command the 6th Royal Scots Fusiliers.

1916 Returned to House of Commons.

1917 Minister of Munitions.

1918 Secretary of State for War and Air.

1921 Colonial Secretary.

1924–1929 Chancellor of Exchequer.

1929 Conservative Member and keen critic of Government's appeasement of Hitler and Mussolini.

1939 First Lord of the Admiralty again.

1940–1945 Prime Minister.

1943 Hon. Academician Extraordinary of the R.A.

1946 Made 'Iron Curtain' Speech, Fulton, Missouri.

1951 Prime Minister again.

1953 Awarded Nobel Prize for Literature; made Knight of the Garter by Queen Elizabeth II.

1963 By Act of Congress, named Honorary Citizen of the United States (first person so honored); resigned from the House of Commons.

1964 Celebrated ninetieth birthday.

1965 Died in London, January 24, 1965.